Challenger SECOND EDITION 2

ADULT READING SERIES

Corea Murphy

New Readers Press

Acknowledgements:

Wigs: Adapted and reprinted with permission from *Hair: The Long and Short of It,* Bill Severn, 1971. Published by David McKay Company, Inc.

A Very Strange Hobby: Adapted with permission from *Incredible Collectors, Weird Antiques and Odd Hobbies,* Bill Carmichael. © 1971 by William E. Carmichael. Published by Prentice-Hall, Inc.

Black Bart (1830–1917): Adapted from "The Case of the Plodding Highwayman or the PO8 of Crime," Pat Kraft. © 1966 American Heritage Publishing Co., Inc. Printed with permission of AHMC, Inc. d/b/a American Heritage Publishing.

Jails on the High Seas: Adapted from "The Galleys of France," W.H. Lewis, pp. 136–145 from *"Essays Presented to Charles Williams"* by Lewis, W.H. (1947) and by permission of Oxford University Press.

The Father of Our Country: Adapted with permission from *Facts About the Presidents,* by Joseph Nathan Kane. © 1959 by The H.W. Wilson Company.

Images courtesy of:

p. 5, p. 10 p. 15, p. 19, p. 20, p. 25, p. 34, p. 39, p. 43, p. 44, p. 50, p. 54 Mother Goose, p. 55 Mother Goose, cow jumping over moon, p. 64, p. 65, p. 69, p. 70, p. 75, p. 76, p. 80, p. 81, p. 84, p. 85, p. 96, p. 97, p. 102, p. 107, p. 108, pp. 113, 119, American Flag: © 2008 Jupiterimages Corporation; p. 47: istockphoto.com; p. 49: p. 54, gravestone, p. 114, p. 119, Washington Crossing the Delaware: Public Domain (Wikimedia Commons); p. 103: Wells Fargo Archives. p. 120; George Washington portrait: The Yorck Project: 10.000 Meisterwerke der Malerei

Challenger 2, 2nd Edition
ISBN 978-1-56420-569-8

Copyright © 2010 New Readers Press
New Readers Press
ProLiteracy's Publishing Division
101 Wyoming Street, Syracuse, New York 13204
www.newreaderspress.com

Printed in the United States of America
9

Proceeds from the sale of New Readers Press materials support professional development, training, and technical assistance programs of ProLiteracy that benefit local literacy programs in the U.S. and around the globe.

Developmental Editor: Terrie Lipke
Contributing Writer: Terry Ledyard
Creative Director: Andrea Woodbury
Production Specialist: Maryellen Casey
Art and Design Supervisor: James P. Wallace
Cover Design: Carolyn Wallace

Table of Contents

Lesson 1
Reading: Sneezing.............................5
Exercises:
    1. About the Reading.........................6
    2. Word Sounds 6
    3. Matching 8
    4. Marking the e's............................8
    5. Words That Sound the Same 9

Lesson 2
Reading: Cats 10
Exercises:
    1. About the Reading.........................11
    2. Word Sounds 11
    3. Putting Words in Classes.................13
    4. Words That Sound the Same 14

Lesson 3
Reading: The Number Seven.....................15
Exercises:
    1. About the Reading.........................16
    2. Word Sounds 16
    3. Number Words..............................18
    4. Word Opposites 18

Lesson 4
Reading: Fun Food Facts.......................19
Exercises:
    1. About the Reading.........................20
    2. Word Sounds 21
    3. Word Sounds 22
    4. Compound Words...........................23
    5. Which Word Does Not Fit?.............24
    6. Smallest and Biggest.....................24

Lesson 5
Reading: Love Letters........................25
Exercises:
    1. About the Reading.........................26
    2. Word Sounds 26
    3. Who Does What? 28
    4. Words That Sound the Same 28
    5. Marking the Vowels.......................29

Review: Lessons 1–5
Word Chart...............................30
Exercises:
    1. Choosing the Answer......................31
    2. Number Words..............................32
    3. Facts......................................32
Word Index: Lessons 1–5 33

Lesson 6
Reading: Wigs 34
Exercises:
    1. About the Reading.........................35
    2. Word Sounds 36
    3. Which Word Does Not Fit?.............37
    4. Vowel Sounds 38
    5. Compound Words...........................38

Lesson 7
Reading: Skunks 39
Exercises:
    1. About the Reading.........................40
    2. Compound Words...........................41
    3. Words That Mean the Same 41
    4. Word Opposites 42
    5. Silly Verses..............................42

Lesson 8
Reading: Eggs 43
Exercises:
    1. About the Reading.........................44
    2. Word Sounds 45
    3. Word Sounds 46
    4. Which Word Fits Best? 47
    5. Compound Words...........................48

Lesson 9
Reading: Gold...............................49
Exercises:
    1. About the Reading.........................50
    2. Word Sounds 51
    3. Vowels + the Letter *l* 52
    4. Marking the Vowels.......................53
    5. Matching 53

Lesson 10
Reading: Mother Goose 54
Exercises:
    1. About the Reading.........................55
    2. Word Sounds 56
    3. Which Word Does Not Fit?.............57
    4. Silent Letters............................58
    5. Words That Sound the Same 59

Review: Lessons 1–10
Word Chart...............................60
Exercises:
    1. Choosing the Answer......................61
    2. Words That Mean the Same 62
    3. Word Opposites 62
Word Index: Lessons 1–10 63

Lesson 11
Reading: Sleeping 64
Exercises:
   1. About the Reading.....................65
   2. Word Sounds 66
   3. Long and Short Vowels 67
   4. Putting Words in Order................68

Lesson 12
Reading: Honeybees 69
Exercises:
   1. About the Reading.....................70
   2. Word Sounds 71
   3. Words That End in -y 72
   4. Words That End in -ly 73
   5. Compound Words......................74
   6. Changing the f to v....................74

Lesson 13
Reading: Handwriting 75
Exercises:
   1. About the Reading.....................76
   2. Words That Mean the Same 78
   3. Word Opposites 78
   4. Vowel Sounds............................79

Lesson 14
Reading: Smoking...............................80
Exercises:
   1. About the Reading.....................81
   2. True or False? 82
   3. Working with Words That Rhyme.....82
   4. Words That End in -er 83

Lesson 15
Reading: A Very Strange Hobby.................84
Exercises:
   1. About the Reading.....................85
   2. Working with Words That Rhyme......86
   3. How Do You Say It? 88

Review: Lessons 1–15
Word Chart..89
Exercises:
   1. Choosing the Answer....................90
   2. Silent Letters.............................91
   3. Matching 92
   4. Word Sounds 93
   5. Compound Words......................93
Word Index: Lessons 1–15 94

Lesson 16
Reading: Whales.................................96
Exercises:
   1. About the Reading.....................97

   2. True or False? 98
   3. Putting Words in Order..................99
   4. Changing the y to i.....................100
   5. More Work with Changing the y to i ..100
   6. Which Word Fits Best? 101

Lesson 17
Reading: Black Bart..............................102
Exercises:
   1. About the Reading.....................103
   2. Words That Mean the Same 104
   3. Word Opposites 105
   4. A Verse from Black Bart 105
   5. The Ending -ful 106

Lesson 18
Reading: Earth Day...............................107
Exercises:
   1. About the Reading.....................108
   2. Word Sounds 109
   3. The Ending -less 110
   4. Same or Opposite? 112
   5. Spelling Check...........................112

Lesson 19
Reading: Jails on the High Seas...............113
Exercises:
   1. About the Reading.....................114
   2. Words That Sound the Same 115
   3. Which Word Does Not Fit?.............116
   4. Words That Begin with un- 117
   5. Common Sayings 118

Lesson 20
Reading: The Father of Our Country..........119
Exercises:
   1. About the Reading.....................120
   2. Vowel Sounds...........................121
   3. Compound Words.......................122
   4. More Work with the Ending -ly 123
   5. More Common Sayings..................124

Review: Lessons 1–20
Exercises:
   1. Words That Mean the Same 125
   2. Word Opposites 125
   3. Twenty Questions 126
   4. Which Word Fits Best? 127
   5. Words That Sound the Same 128
Word Index: Lessons 1–20 130

Word Index: Books 1 and 2.......................132

Answer Key 138

Words for Study

somebody	recorded	September	children
God	Donna	every	sense
cover	Griffiths	ugly	touch
dust	January	Pinocchio	mouth

LESSON 1
Sneezing

At one time or another, everybody sneezes. If somebody hears the sneeze, he might say, "God bless you." Most people cover their noses when they sneeze, so their germs won't go all over the room. Some things that often make people sneeze are dust, pet hair, weeds, black pepper, and colds.

The longest sneezing fit ever recorded was that of a twelve-year-old girl named Donna Griffiths. She started sneezing on January 13, 1981, and didn't stop until September 16, 1983. She sneezed every few minutes for 978 days.

1 About the Reading. Answer these questions.

1. Why do most people cover their noses when they sneeze?

_____

2. What do people often say when they hear somebody sneeze?

_____

3. List three things that can make people sneeze _____

4. How old was Donna Griffiths when she had her sneezing fit?

_____

5. For how many days did Donna Griffiths sneeze? _____

What do you think?

6. Do you sneeze more often in the spring or the fall? _____

2 Word Sounds. Pick the right answer, and fill it in on the line. Then write all three words at the left. Check your answer to make sure it makes sense. Note how the first one has been done.

| c, gr, *or* sh | **1.** Do you like the ___sh___ape of your nose? |

_____ *cape* _____

_____ *grape* _____

_____ *shape* _____

| dr, st, *or* th | **2.** Many people _____ink that their noses are ugly. |

_____

_____

_____

ch, r, _or_ str

_____
_____
_____

3. If you have the money, you can _____ange the shape of your nose.

ch, gr, _or_ kn

_____
_____
_____

4. Pinocchio is a little boy in a children's story. Every time he told a lie, his nose _____ew very long.

cr, dr, _or_ tr

_____
_____
_____

5. Somebody who always _____ies to find out what other people are doing is called nosy.

bl, j, _or_ sn

_____
_____
_____

6. Somebody who walks around with his nose in the air is often called a _____ob.

gr, kn, _or_ sn

_____
_____
_____

7. Do you _____ow anybody who has a very big nose?

Sm, Sp, _or_ Sw

_____
_____
_____

8. _____elling is one of the five senses.

h, l, *or* st

_____

_____

_____

9. Some people sneeze when they _____and in the sun.

bl, p, *or* st

_____

_____

_____

10. People who have _____uffed-up noses from bad colds can't smell well at all.

3 Matching. Match the part of the body with the right sense.

hearing	seeing	smelling	tasting	touching

_____ **1.** ear

_____ **2.** eye

_____ **3.** hand

_____ **4.** mouth

_____ **5.** nose

4 Marking the e's. Mark the e's in these words. If the sound for e is long, put a line over it. If the sound for e is short, put a curved line over it. If you don't hear the e at all, put a line through it.

1. thēse̸

2. ĕnd

3. alone

4. bleed

5. harmless

6. next

7. useful

8. pancake

9. remind

10. sweat

11. close

12. choose

5 Words That Sound the Same. These words sound the same, but they do not have the same meaning. Put the right word on each line.

eye *and* I

1. _____ can't see as well when my right _____ is covered.

hear *and* here

2. Mrs. White did not _____ her child say, "Did you know that Dr. Griffiths is _____?"

two *and* to

3. _____ people won free passes _____ the movies.

dear *and* deer

4. When the little boy heard the gun go off, he said, "Oh _____, I hope the _____ wasn't hurt."

for *and* four

5. When the flames burst from the first floor of the house, _____ children ran _____ help.

knows *and* nose

6. Pinocchio _____ that his _____ will get bigger every time he tells a lie.

Words for Study

dim	sometimes	noise	meow
sharp	doctor	catbird	purr
United States	Canadian	its	relate
country	human	describe	wolves

LESSON 2
Cats

Many people like having cats for house pets. Cats are very smart animals. They can see better in dim light than man or any other animal. Their eyes shine in the dark. Cats also have sharp senses of smell and hearing. However, because cats like to have their own way, it takes longer to train a cat as a pet than it takes to train a dog.

The United States has more cats than any other country. It has been recorded that more than ninety million cats live in the United States.

People who love cats can do strange things sometimes. A doctor on the West Coast, who died in 1963, left $415,000 to his two fifteen-year-old cats in his will. In 2005, a Canadian man left over $1,000,000 to his cat Red.

1 About the Reading. Answer these questions.

1. Which country has the most cats? _____

2. How many cats does this country have? _____

3. How much money did the man on the West Coast leave his two cats?

_____

4. How much money did the Canadian man leave his cat? _____

5. What can a cat do better than man or any other animal?

_____

What do you think?

6. Which do you think make better pets—cats or dogs? Why?

_____

_____

2 Word Sounds. Pick the right answer and fill it in on the line. Then write all three words at the left. Check your answer to make sure it makes sense.

br, gr, *or* st

_____

_____

_____

1. Some people can't _____ and to be around cats because cats make them sneeze.

cr, j, *or* b

_____

_____

_____

2. Others don't like to be around cats because these animals give them the _____ eeps.

dr, tr, or br

_____

_____

3. A cat's _____ain is more like a human's _____ain than a dog's _____ain.

wr, str, or l

_____

_____

4. Cats have a very _____ong sense of hearing. They hear noises that even dogs can't hear.

dr, gl, or st

_____

_____

5. Cats begin _____eaming when they are only about one week old.

b, sl, or bl

_____

_____

6. In some countries _____ack cats are thought to be lucky, and in other countries they are thought of as unlucky.

br, cl, or cr

_____

_____

7. A catbird has a black _____own and tail and makes a sound like that of a cat.

sl, sh, or st

_____

_____

_____

8. Cats _____eep 16–18 hours a day.

s, h, *or* tr

_____

_____

_____

9. When well _____eated, a cat can live twenty years or more.

s, sp, *or* t

_____

_____

_____

10. The biggest fish that _____ends its whole life in fresh water is a catfish.

3 Putting Words in Classes. Put the words that describe cats in **List A.** Put the words that describe dogs in **List B.**

barking	always land on their feet	man's best friend
meowing	chasing cars	nine lives	climbing trees
purring	digging up bones	related to wolves

List A: Cats

1. _____

2. _____

3. _____

4. _____

5. _____

List B: Dogs

1. _____

2. _____

3. _____

4. _____

5. _____

4 Words That Sound the Same. Put the right word on each line.

buy *and* **by**

1. _____ the time Min-hee got through shopping, she had no money left to _____ food for dinner.

knew *and* **new**

2. Ben _____ a man who would tear up his work and start all over on a _____ page even if he made only one mistake.

ate *and* **eight**

3. When Dave got home from work last night, he _____ _____ hot dogs for dinner.

do *and* **due**

4. "_____ you know what time the plane is _____?" asked Mary.

hour *and* **our**

5. "_____ plane should be here in an _____," said her aunt.

Words for Study

everywhere	sins	mentioned	temple
seas	Snow White	Bible	craps
world	dwarves	King Solomon	break
deadly	Seven Up	built	mirror

6, 8, 9 good in China 4 not good

LESSON 3
The Number Seven

The number seven is everywhere. There are seven days in a week. There are seven seas and seven wonders of the world. There are seven deadly sins. Snow White had seven dwarves.

There is a soft drink called 7UP. Seven Up is even the name of a children's card game. Seven is mentioned in the Bible many times. God is said to have made the world in seven days. King Solomon built a temple. It took him seven years.

Is there something lucky about the number seven? Many people think so. Go to any casino. In some games a score of seven wins. Craps is one of those games. Lucky seven wins!

But seven can be unlucky, too. If you break a mirror, some people say you will have seven years of bad luck.

1 About the Reading. Answer these questions.

1. What did Snow White have seven of? _____

2. What is the name of a soft drink and a children's card game? _____

3. What does the Bible say God made in seven days? _____

4. How long did it take King Solomon to build his temple? _____

5. What casino game can you win with a score of seven? _____

6. What do some people think will happen if you break a mirror?

_____

2 Word Sounds. Pick the right answer, and fill it in on the line. Then write all three words at the left. Check your answer to make sure it makes sense.

bl, g, *or* fl

_____

_____

_____

1. Seven Up is the name of a children's card _____ame.

bl, dr, *or* st

_____

_____

_____

2. It is also the name of a soft _____ink.

Cr, Sn, *or* Cl

_____

_____

_____

3. _____aps is a dice game often played in casinos.

bl, dr, *or* th

_____

_____

4. Do you _____ink that you will have seven years of bad luck if you break a mirror?

thr, kn, *or* bl

_____

_____

5. Do you _____ow the story of Snow White and the Seven Dwarves?

kn, n, *or* f

_____

_____

6. Have you seen the _____ew list of seven wonders of the world?

ch, p, *or* w

_____

_____

7. The seventh day of the _____eek is Saturday.

br, pr, *or* h

_____

_____

8. One of the seven deadly sins is _____ide.

pl, f, *or* r

_____

_____

9. Las Vegas is a _____ace known for its casinos.

3 Number Words. Read these number words.

twenty (20)	twenty-eight (28)	seventy (70)
twenty-one (21)	twenty-nine (29)	eighty (80)
twenty-two (22)	thirty (30)	ninety (90)
twenty-three (23)	thirty-one (31)	one hundred (100)
twenty-four (24)	forty (40)	one thousand (1,000)
twenty-five (25)	fifty (50)	one million (1,000,000)
twenty-six (26)	sixty (60)	one billion (1,000,000,000)
twenty-seven (27)		

Answer these questions by writing the words for the numbers on the line.

_____ 1. How many hours are in a day?

_____ 2. How many days are in the month of January?

_____ 3. How many days are in the month of June?

_____ 4. How many states are in the United States?

_____ 5. How many hours a week do most people work at their jobs?

_____ 6. How old were you on your last birthday?

Do you know?

_____ 7. By law, how old do you have to be to drive a car?

_____ 8. By law, how old do you have to be to vote?

4 Word Opposites. Match each word below with the word that means the opposite. The first one has been done for you.

break	✓go	many	something
everybody	in	soft	win

_____go_____ 1. come _____ 5. lose

_____ 2. few _____ 6. nobody

_____ 3. fix _____ 7. nothing

_____ 4. hard _____ 8. out

Words for Study

pizza	squid	half	tomatoes
person	potato	cereals	sauce
pepperoni	vegetable	sugar	strawberries
Japan	pounds	grown	fruit

LESSON 4
Fun Food Facts

What food do you like best? If you said pizza, you are not alone. Pizza is a much-loved food in the United States. People buy about three billion pizzas each year. That's about 46 slices for every person! What tops it most often? Pepperoni. In Japan, squid tops most pizzas.

The potato is the top vegetable in the United States. Each person eats about 140 pounds every year. About half are fresh potatoes. The rest are eaten in foods like French fries.

Here are some more fun food facts:

- It takes about ten pounds of milk to make one pound of cheese.

- Popcorn was one of the first breakfast cereals. People put sugar and milk on it.

- Corn and rice are grown by farmers all over the world. But corn is the most grown crop in the whole world.

- Each person in the United States eats about 22 pounds of tomatoes every year. More than half are eaten as ketchup or tomato sauce.

- Strawberries are the only fruit with seeds on the outside. And they have little sugar in them.

- Grapes are one of the oldest grown fruits. They have been around for more than 8,000 years.

1 About the Reading. Answer these questions.

1. How many pizzas do people in the United States buy each year?

_____

2. In the United States, what tops pizza most often? _____

3. In what country does squid top pizza the most? _____

4. How many pounds of potatoes does each person in the United States eat every year? _____

5. How are all those potatoes eaten? _____

6. What does it take 10 pounds of milk to make? _____

7. What was one of the first breakfast cereals? _____

8. What is the only fruit with seeds on the outside? _____

9. Over half of the tomatoes eaten each year are eaten as what foods?

_____

10. What fruit has been around for more than 8,000 years? _____

What do you think?

11. What do you like on top of your pizza? _____

12. How do you eat potatoes? _____

2 Word Sounds. Pick the right answer, and fill it in on the line. Then write all three words at the left. Check your answer to make sure it makes sense.

ch, r, or str

_____

_____

1. There are many _____ange records about food.

p, m, or h

_____

_____

2. The record for the _____ost pancakes made in eight hours is 34,818.

scr, dr, or cr

_____

_____

3. In 2007, a man made 19 ice-_____eam cones in one minute.

f, p, or s

_____

_____

4. Can you believe that somebody ate one _____ound of grapes (with seeds) in sixty-five seconds?

f, sp, or k

_____

_____

5. The largest bowl of cereal was _____illed with over 2,000 pounds of cornflakes.

sh, str, or sw

_____

_____

6. The record for eating _____eet corn is held by a man who ate 34.75 ears in 12 minutes.

ch, thr, *or* bl

7. In 2006, a TV host _____ew a pancake 14 feet in the air.

_____

_____

_____

pr, sp, *or* sl

8. One man ate 45 _____ices of pizza in only 12 minutes.

_____

_____

_____

3 Word Sounds. Fill in the right word on each line. Then check your answers to make sure they make sense. Note how the first one has been done.

chairs pair stairs

1. The top of the _____ *stairs* _____ was blocked by a _____ *pair* _____ of _____ *chairs* _____.

cloud loudly proud

2. Dave was so _____ of the _____ he drew in art class that he said _____, "Hey, everybody, look at my picture!"

brave cave waves

3. The boys tried to be _____ as the _____ came crashing into the _____.

cried dried tried

4. After Sue _____, she _____ to stay by herself until her tears _____.

clear hear near

5. Min-hee did not _____ her aunt ask her to _____ off the chair that was _____ the front door.

change range strange	**6.** Cowboys riding on the _____ sometimes think that a _____ in the sky is _____.
beans mean jeans	**7.** The cowboy didn't _____ to spill _____ all over his _____.
bunch lunch munched	**8.** Eddie didn't have time to eat _____ on Thursday, so he _____ on a _____ of grapes while he worked.
bricks stick trick	**9.** Jack thought there must be a _____ to getting the _____ to _____ to each other in just the right way.
cape grape shape	**10.** The _____ of the _____ made Mary's head look like a _____.

4 Compound Words. A compound word is made up of two or more smaller words. Find the two words that make up each compound word, and write them on the lines. Note how the first one has been done.

1. popcorn   ___*pop*___ + ___*corn*___   **6.** grapefruit _____ + _____

2. fruitcake _____ + _____   **7.** strawberry _____ + _____

3. breakfast _____ + _____   **8.** somebody _____ + _____

4. outside _____ + _____   **9.** everywhere _____ + _____

5. blueberries _____ + _____   **10.** cookbook _____ + _____

5 Which Word Does Not Fit? Use the first word to help you choose the word in the line that does not fit. The first one has been done for you.

1. meal: breakfast   lunch   dinner   snack   <u>snack</u>

2. vegetable: corn   potato   pear   beet   _____

3. fruit: grape   candy   strawberry   fig   _____

4. countries: Japan   United States   world   Canada   _____

5. animals: catbirds   wolves   squid   pets   _____

6. food: pound   pizza   tomato   milk   _____

7. job: farmer   nurse   mall   bus driver   _____

6 Smallest and Biggest. In each set of words, which is the smallest? Write the answer on the line to the left. Which is the biggest? Write the answer on the line to the right. The first set has been done for you.

Smallest		Biggest
<u>week</u>	1. week, year, or month	<u>year</u>
_____	2. million, thousand, or billion	_____
_____	3. tomato, grape, or potato	_____
_____	4. Japan, United States, or world	_____
_____	5. whole, half, or third	_____
_____	6. none, many, or few	_____
_____	7. baby, grown-up, or child	_____
_____	8. ounce, pound, or ton	_____

Words for Study

letter	paper	chain	vowel
written	surely	well-known	remember
lover	reason	either	cowboy
scribe	John	important	tailor
instead	copy	alphabet	sail

LESSON 5
Love Letters

The strangest love letter ever written was the work of a French painter in 1875. The only thing written in the letter was "I love you." What is strange about that? "I love you" was written 1,875,000 times—a thousand times the year of the date!

The lover did not write this letter himself. He hired a scribe to do it for him. A scribe is a person who writes letters and other things for a living.

This painter didn't just tell the scribe to write a letter saying "I love you" 1,875,000 times. This would have been too easy.

Instead, the lover stayed right there with the scribe and said "I love you" 1,875,000 times. Each time he said it, the scribe had to write these three words down on paper. Surely, this must have been the most boring job that this scribe ever had!

1 About the Reading. Answer these questions.

1. In what year did the French painter hire somebody to write a love letter for him?

_____

2. What do you call a person hired to write or copy something for somebody else?

_____

3. How many times did the scribe have to write "I love you" on paper?

_____

4. If you were the French painter and you hired a scribe to write this letter in 2010, how many times would the scribe have to write "I love you"? _____

What do you think?

5. What do you think the woman who got this letter thought of her lover?

_____

6. Give a reason that explains why people wrote more letters in the 1800s than they write today. _____

2 Word Sounds. Choose the right word, and fill it in on the line.

selling
spelling
telling

1. A letter that a woman writes to a man _____ him that she no longer loves him is called a "Dear John" letter.

classed
massed
passed

2. A letter that is copied and then _____ on to somebody else to read is called a chain letter.

mail nail tail	**3.** Letters that well-known people get from those who really like their work are called fan _____.
knife life wife	**4.** A red-letter day is a day that has been either a very happy day or a very important day in your _____.
fix mix six	**5.** There are twenty-_____ letters in the English alphabet.
bore more store	**6.** The letter e is used _____ often than any other letter of the alphabet.
towels vowels	**7.** *A, E, I, O,* and *U* are called _____.
much such	**8.** In English, there is no _____ thing as a word without a vowel sound in it.
skill spill still	**9.** Can you _____ sing the song that you learned as a child to help you remember all the letters of the alphabet?
long song wrong	**10.** The _____ sounds like this: "A, B, C, D, E, F, G, H, I, J, K, L, M, N, O, P, Q, R, S, T, U, V, W, X, Y, and Z. Now I know my A B C's. Next time won't you sing with me?"

3 Who Does What? Choose the right answer, and write it on the line. Note how the first one has been done.

> cowboy   doctor   painter   clown
> baseball player
>   ✓cab driver
> lover   scribe   tailor   teacher

1. A _____cab driver_____ drives people where they want to go.

2. A _____ gets base hits.

3. A _____ helps people to learn.

4. A _____ helps people who are sick.

5. A _____ herds cows on the range.

6. A _____ makes and mends clothes.

7. A _____ makes people laugh.

8. A _____ paints pictures.

9. A _____ can be a boyfriend or girlfriend.

10. A _____ writes letters for other people.

4 Words That Sound the Same. Put the right word on each line.

right *and* write   **1.** Bob could not _____ with his _____ hand after he smashed it in the car door.

hole *and* whole   **2.** The dog ran off with the _____ bone and hid it in a _____ behind the house.

beat *and* beet	**3.** The mother _____ the dust from the bed until her face got as red as a _____.
fair *and* fare	**4.** People did not think that the new bus _____ was _____.
meat *and* meet	**5.** The women would _____ each other at the store and talk about the high price of _____.
heard *and* herd	**6.** The cowboy said, "Have you _____ that the _____ will sell for a higher price this year?"
sails *and* sale	**7.** Ben read in the paper that there was a _____ on _____ at the boat shop down at the dock.
one *and* won	**8.** It was the middle of June, and Becky had not _____ _____ baseball game yet.

5 Marking the Vowels. Mark the vowels in these words either long or short. If you don't hear the vowel at all, draw a line through it.

1. frāmé

2. brănd

3. known

4. pint

5. state

6. sins

7. sense

8. catbird

9. squid

10. relate

11. spice

12. wrote

Review: Lessons 1-5

Say these words out loud.					
charm	chart	smart	smoke	choke	check
drew	draw	straw	stroke	broke	break
germ	term	team	steam	stain	chain
purr	puff	stuff	step	stop	chop
skirt	skill	shrill	shrink	shrunk	skunk
slang	sleep	creep	crumb	thumb	numb
ail	pail	rail	sail	tail	
ban	band	brand	grand	stand	
cheek	peek	seek	week		
bend	lend	mend	spend	tend	
brick	lick	pick	stick	trick	
blink	drink	ink	sink	stink	
blown	grown	known	own		

1 Choosing the Answer. Choose the right word, and fill it in on the line.

1. There are _____ states in the United States.

a. forty   b. forty-nine   c. fifty   d. fifty-two

2. The speaker gave a _____ on Japan that lasted for over an hour.

a. tail   b. tale   c. talk   d. tall

3. Dave couldn't make any _____ out of the words Min-hee had written on the paper.

a. send   b. sense   c. sent   d. seen

4. Joan would never buy clothes that had too much _____ on them because they were too hard to take care of.

a. lace   b. lake   c. lame   d. lane

5. After seven years of married life, Becky was still very much in love with her _____.

a. made   b. make   c. male   d. mate

6. John didn't _____ to hurt the child's feelings.

a. meal   b. mean   c. meat   d. met

7. When Kate returned from lunch, she had a huge _____ of ketchup on her brand-new dress.

a. blob   b. bob   c. mob   d. sob

8. When Eddie kissed Kate, she was sure she was _____.

a. bleeding   b. blessing   c. bluffing   d. blushing

9. Louise didn't remember to _____ her book, so she had to pay a small fine.

a. react   b. refund   c. refuse   d. renew

10. As Bob drank the water from the pond, he told June, "Don't make such a fuss. The water is not _____."

    a. deadly   b. loudly   c. firmly   d. surely

2 Number Words. Answer these questions by writing the word for the number. Get a friend to help you if you wish. Some of these questions are hard!

_____ **1.** How many days are in a week?

_____ **2.** How many weeks are in a year?

_____ **3.** How many ounces are in a pound?

_____ **4.** How many ounces are in a cup?

_____ **5.** How many cups are in a pint?

_____ **6.** How many pints are in a quart?

_____ **7.** How many quarts are in a gallon?

_____ **8.** How many stripes are on the United States flag?

_____ **9.** How many stars are on the United States flag?

_____ **10.** According to some people, how many years of bad luck will you have if you break a mirror?

_____ **11.** What is your lucky number?

_____ **12.** What is one hundred times ten?

3 Facts. List the five senses.

1. _____   **4.** _____

2. _____   **5.** _____

3. _____

Word Index: Lessons 1–5

A
alphabet

B
ban
bend
berry
Bible
billion
blink
blob
blown
blueberry
bluff
brand
brand-new
break
brick
build
built
bunch

C
Canada
Canadian
catbird
catfish
cave
cereal
chain
change
cheek
children
choke
cloud
compound
copy
cornflakes
country
cover
cowboy
craps
creep

D
deadly
describe
dim
doctor
Donna
drank
draw
drew
dust
dwarves

E
eighty
either
English
every
everywhere

F
feeling
frame
fruit
fruitcake

G
gallon
God
grand
grapefruit
grew
Griffiths
grow
grown
grown-up

H
half
hey
host
human
hundred

I
important
instead
its

J
January

Japan
John

K
kill
King Solomon

L
Las Vegas
letter
lover

M
mass
meaning
mention
meow
mirror
mouth
munch

N
noise

O

P
pail
paper
pepperoni
person

Pinocchio
pint
pizza
post
potato
pound
puff
purr

Q
quart

R
rail
react
reason
record
relate
remember
renew

S
sail
sauce
saying
scribe
sea
sense
September
seventh
seventy

Seven Up
sharp
sheep
sheet
shrill
sin
slack
slang
snack
snap
snob
Snow White
somebody
sometimes
speaker
spell
spice
squid
stand
state
steam
stick
stink
strawberry
sugar
surely
swell

T
tailor
team
temple

tend
term
thousand
tomato
ton
touch
towel
trick

U
ugly
United States

V
vegetable
vowel

W
well-known
wolves
world
written

X

Y

Z

LESSON 6
Wigs

Have you ever heard a very important person called a *bigwig?* This term dates back to at least 4000 BC. At that time, both men and women in Egypt shaved their heads and wore wigs. The bigger the wig was, the more important the person was.

One of the reasons that wigs were worn in Egypt was so people could keep their heads clean and free from lice. The wigs were made of many things such as wool, animal hair, and even gold. People used beeswax to make the wigs stick to their heads.

It was not just the people in Egypt who liked to wear wigs. In 1624, when the King of France began to lose his hair at a very early age, he got everybody to wear wigs. Under Queen Anne of England, who ruled from 1702 to 1714, wigs grew to their biggest shapes. They covered people's backs and hung down over their chests.

1 About the Reading. Answer these questions.

1. Name three things the people in Egypt used to make their wigs.

_____   _____   _____

2. What did the people in Egypt use to make their wigs stick to their heads?

_____

3. Why did the king of France in this story start to wear a wig?

_____

4. Describe the wigs that were worn during Queen Anne's time.

_____

5. How many years did Queen Anne rule England? _____

6. How did the term *bigwig* get started?

_____

What do you think?

7. Do people still fuss as much with their hair now as they did a long time ago? Be sure to give a reason for your answer.

_____

_____

2 Word Sounds. Choose the right word, and fill it in on the line.

brave grave shave	**1.** When people _____ their heads, they are bald.
bangs fangs gangs	**2.** Mary had her _____ cut so she could see better.
chair hair pair	**3.** Most wigs that are worn today look just like human _____.
phone stone throne	**4.** The king and queen each had their own _____ to sit on.
rich which witch	**5.** There are many sayings in _____ the word *hair* is used.
Feeling Kneeling Peeling	**6.** _____ really relaxed is called "letting one's hair down."
Fighting Lighting Sighting	**7.** _____ with somebody over something that is not very important is called "splitting hairs."
bugs dug hugs	**8.** When somebody _____ you, he is "getting in your hair."
grand sand stand	**9.** If something really scares you, it "makes your hair _____ on end."

3 Which Word Does Not Fit? Put the word that does not fit with the rest on the line to the right. Note how the first one has been done.

1. January   June   May   month   _____month_____

2. England   English   France   United States   _____

3. catbird   catfish   eel   whale   _____

4. ink   paper   pen   scribe   _____

5. star   kite   start   sun   _____

6. Andy   Anne   Jack   John   _____

7. chair   queen   seat   throne   _____

8. cheek   lip   mouth   wrist   _____

9. ailing   well   ill   sick   _____

10. gallon   pint   pound   quart   _____

4 Vowel Sounds. If the sound for *ea* in the word is long, put the word in the first list. If the sound for *ea* is short, put the word in the second list. Note how the first one has been done.

✓bean	bread	dead	instead	squeal
beat	breakfast	easy	please	sweat

Long Sound for *ea*

1. _bean_
2. _____
3. _____
4. _____
5. _____

Short Sound for *ea*

1. _____
2. _____
3. _____
4. _____
5. _____

5 Compound Words. Find the two little words that make up each compound word, and write them on the lines. Note how the first one has been done.

1. bathroom   _bath_ + _room_
2. bigwig   _____ + _____
3. cowboy   _____ + _____
4. catbird   _____ + _____
5. checkbook   _____ + _____
6. someone   _____ + _____
7. gingerbread   _____ + _____
8. girlfriend   _____ + _____
9. shortstop   _____ + _____
10. sunlight   _____ + _____

Words for Study

bloodstream	spray	tip	refilled
pouches	whatever	shoots	grin
liquid	stamps	rounds	dash
hidden	forefeet	sideways	coins
he's	raises	trouble	shower

LESSON 7
Skunks

A skunk's bad smell is not in his bloodstream or his breath. Under the skunk's tail are two pouches which are filled with liquid. These pouches remain hidden as long as everything is calm. However, when the skunk feels he's in danger, he lifts his tail.

A skunk will not spray the liquid in these pouches unless he feels he's being chased. If chased, the first thing a skunk will do is turn to face whatever is chasing him. Then he stamps his forefeet and raises all of his tail but the tip. If the skunk feels he's still in danger, he raises the tip, snaps his tail into the shape of the letter U, and shoots.

The skunk can fire the liquid from a range of ten to twelve feet. This liquid can be smelled for more than a mile. Each pouch has enough liquid for five or six rounds. A skunk can fire his liquid sideways, straight, and up with no trouble at all. After he fires all his liquid, the skunk has to wait a few days for his pouches to be refilled.

1 About the Reading. Answer these questions.

1. Where does the liquid that a skunk sprays come from?

_____

2. From what range can a skunk spray his liquid?

_____

3. After the skunk sprays his liquid, how long must he wait before he can spray again? _____

4. Why does a skunk spray his liquid?

_____

5. When a skunk feels he's in danger, list three things that he does.

    a. _____

    b. _____

    c. _____

Do you know?

6. If your pet or you are sprayed by a skunk, how do you get rid of the smell?

_____

2 Compound Words. Find the two words that make up each compound word, and write them on the lines.

1. bedroom   _____ + _____

2. bloodstream   _____ + _____

3. troublemaker   _____ + _____

4. homework   _____ + _____

5. teabag   _____ + _____

6. notebook   _____ + _____

7. sideways   _____ + _____

8. someone   _____ + _____

9. catfish   _____ + _____

10. whatever   _____ + _____

3 Words That Mean the Same. Match each word below with the word that means the same. Note how the first one has been done.

| bluff | creep | hidden | sprint | trouble |
| build | grin | nice | touch | ✓wreck |

_____wreck_____   1. break   _____   6. fool

_____   2. covered   _____   7. kind

_____   3. crawl   _____   8. make

_____   4. dash   _____   9. problem

_____   5. feel   _____   10. smile

4 Word Opposites. Match each word below with the word that means the opposite. Note how the first one has been done.

| find | hard | lovely | nothing | shrink |
| forget | late | ✓old | saved | shut |

_____old_____ **1.** brand-new   _____ **6.** lose

_____ **2.** early   _____ **7.** open

_____ **3.** easy   _____ **8.** remember

_____ **4.** everything   _____ **9.** spent

_____ **5.** grow   _____ **10.** ugly

5 Silly Verses. Choose the right word from each set, and fill it in on the line.

cry
dates
sky
state
straight

1. A cowboy who lives in our _____

Is well-known for shooting so _____.

He shoots coins from the _____.

It makes the girls _____.

They ask him to take them on _____.

cried
dance
France
pants
tried

2. There once was a king of _____,

Who couldn't fit into his _____.

He tried and he _____.

Then he broke down and _____.

He couldn't even go to the _____.

hour
life
shower
sour
wife

3. When everything seems to turn _____,

John waits for a better _____.

He gives thanks for his _____,

For his kids and his _____,

And then goes to take a hot _____.

Words for Study

dozen	move	spoil	float
form	breathe	kept	chicken
eggshell	microwave	warm	yolk
tiny	refrigerator	teaspoons	guide

LESSON 8

Eggs

The United States puts out a lot of eggs—75 billion each year. That's about 6.25 billion dozen. There are about 295 million hens. Each lays about 250 to 300 eggs in a year.

How long does it take to make an egg? It takes 24 to 26 hours for a hen to make an egg. About 30 minutes after an egg comes out, another egg begins to form.

Each person eats about 256 eggs each year. Some people eat eggs in the morning for breakfast. Some eggs are eaten hard-boiled. Some are eaten with toast or with ham. Many of the eggs people eat are in other foods.

Eggshells have many tiny holes. They can have more than 20,000 of them. The holes let water and gas move out of the egg. They let in air. The egg can breathe!

You can cook eggs in the microwave, but not in their shells. The steam builds up too quickly. The tiny holes can't let it out fast enough, and the egg can blow up.

Raw eggs will last a long time in the refrigerator. They will stay fresh for about three weeks. But eggs can spoil quickly if they are not kept cold. Warm eggs age more in one day than cold eggs do in one week.

How can you test an egg to see if it is fresh? Put two teaspoons of salt in a cup of water. Then put in the egg. A fresh egg will sink, but an old egg will float.

1 About the Reading. Answer these questions.

1. How many eggs does the United States put out each year? _____

2. How long does each egg take to make? _____

3. How many eggs does each person eat in a year? _____

4. What are some ways people eat eggs? _____

5. Eggshells have thousands of _____.

6. How do eggs breathe? _____

_____

7. What can happen if you cook eggs in their shells in the microwave?

_____

8. How long will raw eggs stay fresh in the refrigerator? _____

9. How can you test an egg to see if it is fresh? _____

_____

Do you know?

10. There is an age-old question about the egg. It asks, "Which came first, the chicken or the egg?" What do you think? Why?

_____

_____

2 Word Sounds. Choose the right answer, and fill it in on the line. Then write all three words at the left. Check your answer to make sure it makes sense.

l, p, or s

_____

_____

_____

1. One hen can _____ay 250–300 eggs each year.

sh, sm, or sp

_____

_____

_____

2. The biggest egg recorded had a double yolk and double _____ell.

sp, gr, or th

_____

_____

_____

3. A hard-cooked egg will _____in, but a raw egg will not.

b, k, or wh

_____

_____

_____

4. Babies can eat the yolks of eggs before they can eat the _____ite part.

br, gr, or ch

_____

_____

_____

5. Laying hens eat a mix of _____ains.

f, m, or p

_____

_____

_____

6. The saying "to lay an egg" means to _____ail at something.

b, d *or* j	**7.** To "put all your eggs in one basket" is to risk everything you have on _____ust one thing.
_____	
_____	

ch, sp, *or* br	**8.** In 2007, a man _____oke a record by holding 20 eggs in one hand.
_____	
_____	

c, gl, *or* sc	**9.** A person who acts _____ared a lot is sometimes called a "chicken."
_____	
_____	

y, cl, *or* f	**10.** The world's oldest chicken lived to be more than 20 _____ears old.
_____	
_____	

3 Word Sounds. Read the words with double *o* below, and put them where they should go. Use the word at the top of each list to guide you. Note how the first one has been done.

✓foot	hood	shoot	took	wood
groom	pool	spoon	tooth	wool

Book

1. _____foot_____

2. _____

3. _____

4. _____

School

1. _____

2. _____

3. _____

4. _____

4 Which Word Fits Best? Choose the word which fits best, and write it on the line. Note how the first one has been done.

1. Meat is to plate as milk is to __*glass*_____.
   a. glass   b. jug   c. liquid   d. white

2. Ship is to sea as plane is to _____.
   a. fast   b. land   c. sky   d. wings

3. Bread is to loaf as cigarettes are to _____.
   a. can   b. jar   c. pack   d. smoke

4. Microwave is to heat as refrigerator is to _____.
   a. food   b. oven   c. cook   d. chill

5. French is to France as English is to _____.
   a. Canada   b. England   c. reading   d. school

6. March is to month as _____ is to day.
   a. hour   b. January   c. Wednesday   d. week

7. Shower is to bathroom as _____ is to living room.
   a. chair   b. door   c. lightbulb   d. sink

8. Hand is to arm as _____ is to leg.
   a. arm   b. body   c. foot   d. knee

9. Park is to play as _____ is to learn.
   a. books   b. class   c. reading   d. school

10. Mouth is to food as _____ is to air.
   a. body   b. blood   c. breath   d. lung

5 Compound Words. Choose a word in **List A**, and add a word from **List B** to it to make a compound word. Note how the first one has been done.

List A	List B
✓arm	bow
baby	✓chair
egg	down
fore	feet
grand	shell
life	sit
rain	stand
some	time
touch	times

1. _____armchair_____

2. _____

3. _____

4. _____

5. _____

6. _____

7. _____

8. _____

9. _____

Put the compound words you have written in these sentences. Note how the compound word _armchair_ has been used.

10. A _____ in football is worth six points.

11. Kate checked each egg to make sure the _____ wasn't broken.

12. _____ I like to take a walk after dinner.

13. We got seats in the _____ to hear the band play.

14. Min-hee wanted to buy a new _____**armchair**_____ for her living room.

15. When the skunk started stamping his _____, we ran.

16. The mother needed someone to _____ her children.

17. Do you think there is a pot of gold at the end of the _____?

18. Dan said his trip to England was the chance of a _____.

Words for Study

California	dollars	lonely	isn't
Sutter	worth	shacks	glitters
news	forty-niners	boots	Jill
miner	wherever	El Dorado	chocolate
between	dusty	common	peach

LESSON 9
Gold

In January 1848, gold was found in California. The gold was found on land owned by John A. Sutter. He tried very hard to keep the good news from getting out, but by May miners were streaming in.

A few men found between 300 and 500 dollars worth of gold dust a day. However, most of the miners panned one ounce of gold dust each day, which was worth about twenty dollars. Workers back East were making only a dollar a day then. So twenty dollars was a lot of money to these men.

The real gold rush began in 1849 when 100,000 men from all over the world rushed to California to strike it rich. These men were called the "forty-niners." They lived in mining camps which formed wherever somebody had made a strike. These camps had only one street. The street was very dusty during the dry spells and very muddy when the rains came.

Men would work hard all day digging for gold and then return to their lonely shacks at night. They would fix a meal of beans, fried bread, and coffee. It was rare to see a woman in one of these mining towns. Some men would pay a dollar just to look at a pair of women's boots.

1 About the Reading. Answer these questions.

1. In which state did the gold rush happen? _____

2. On what man's land was the gold first found? _____

3. In what year did the real gold rush begin? _____

4. What were the men called who came to California to strike it rich?

_____

5. How many ounces of gold dust did most of the miners find each day?

_____

6. Why would men pay a dollar just to see a pair of women's boots?

_____

What do you think?

7. If you had been living in 1849, would you have rushed to California to find gold? Explain your answer.

_____

_____

2 Word Sounds. Pick the right answer, and fill it in on the line. Then write all three words at the left. Check your answer to make sure it makes sense.

br, d, *or* spr _____ _____ _____	**1.** In the 1500s, a story _____ead about a land rich in gold that was called El Dorado.
b, f, *or* th _____ _____ _____	**2.** People _____ought that gold was as common as sand in El Dorado.
bl, f, *or* m _____ _____ _____	**3.** Through the years, many men set out to _____ind El Dorado, and they often thought they had found it.
f, c, *or* p _____ _____ _____	**4.** A rock that looks like gold but isn't gold at all is called _____ool's gold.
l, cl, *or* m _____ _____ _____	**5.** Do you know what the saying "All that glitters is not gold"_____eans?
c, g, *or* h _____ _____ _____	**6.** An ounce of _____old today would sell for over 700 dollars.

sh, st, *or* sc

_____

_____

_____

7. When miners found gold, _____ores raised the prices of things the miners needed.

fr, tr, *or* thr

_____

_____

_____

8. By 1851, miners were paying _____ee dollars for just one egg.

3 Vowels + the Letter *l*. Use the words below to fill in the lines in the sentences.

bald	belt	cold	hill	milk	tall
bell	bulb	gold	Jill	roll	wall

1. A _____ helps to keep your pants up.

2. Are you short or _____?

3. Children are told to let the ball _____ when it goes into the street.

4. Many children are told to drink four glasses of _____ a day.

5. Men in 1849 looked for _____ in California.

6. The light _____ did not fit in the lamp.

7. The pictures hanging on the _____ were lovely.

8. When the _____ rang, everybody came in for lunch.

9. When you have a bad _____, you sneeze a lot.

10. When you have no hair on your head, you are _____.

11. Jack and _____ went up the _____ to fetch a pail of water.

4 Marking the Vowels. Mark the vowels that have lines under them. Note how the first two words have been done.

1. līc̵e

6. r_ea_son

11. Fr_a_nc̵e

15. h_a_lf

2. kĕpt

7. r_ai_se

12. br_a_ke

16. t_i_p

3. d_a_sh

8. gr_a_ve

13. betw_ee_n

17. s_i_nce

4. gl_i_tter

9. ch_ee_k

14. j_u_st

18. br_ea_the

5. fl_oa_t

10. t_e_st

5 Matching. Match each word below with the words that best describe it.

bigwig chocolate	coffee kneel	lice March	microwave news	peach yolk

_____ **1.** a hot, strong, black drink

_____ **2.** a fruit that grows on trees

_____ **3.** a sweet used in candy or drinks

_____ **4.** a very important person

_____ **5.** the middle of an egg

_____ **6.** the third month of the year

_____ **7.** to get down on your knees

_____ **8.** very small bugs that bite the skin of people and animals

_____ **9.** stories you read in the paper

_____ **10.** a very fast oven

goose	proof	fiddle	sport
though	rhymes	lapdog	blackbird
claim	example	ladies	stuck
graveyard	tease	soup	elm
Boston	lords	diddle	silent

LESSON 10
Mother Goose

Mother Goose was not a real person even though some people claim that she was. In an old graveyard in Boston, there are many graves bearing the name *Goose*. Some people think that one of these graves was for Mother Goose, but there is no proof that this is really so.

One of the earliest books of Mother Goose rhymes and stories for children was printed in 1760. Many of these rhymes had been around for hundreds of years. They were not always called Mother Goose rhymes. Some of the rhymes have no real meaning, but others were written about real people.

For example, one queen of England loved to tease her lords the way a cat plays with mice. She also loved to dance to tunes played on a fiddle. One of her lords was nicknamed "Moon." Another lord was known as the Queen's "lapdog."

This queen never ate her soup without having someone taste it first. One of her ladies-in-waiting was called "Spoon" because she tasted the soup.

HERE LYES Y BODY OF
MARY GOOSE WIFE TO
ISAAC GOOSE AGED 42
YEARS DEC.D OCTOBER
19 1690
Here lyef alfo fufana
goofe aged 15 m°

The man who carried the soup was called "Dish." When Dish and Spoon ran off to get married, somebody in the queen's court made up this rhyme:

Hey diddle, diddle,
The cat and the fiddle,
The cow jumped over the moon;
The little dog laughed
To see such sport
And the dish ran away with the spoon.

1 About the Reading. Answer these questions.

1. In what city in the United States do some people think Mother Goose lived?

_____

2. In what year was an early Mother Goose book printed? _____

3. Do all the rhymes tell about real people? _____

4. What was Dish's job? _____

5. What was Spoon's job? _____

6. What happened to Dish and Spoon? _____

7. What fact in the story tells us that Mother Goose did not write these rhymes shortly before 1760? _____

_____

What do you think?

8. Why do children like to hear Mother Goose rhymes? _____

_____

2 Word Sounds. Can you end these lines from well-known rhymes? Pick the right answer, and fill it in on the line. Then write all three words at the left. (Get a friend to help if you do not know all the rhymes.)

  1. Little Boy Blue come blow your _____orn.

_____

_____

_____

b, c, or h

d, p, or t **2.** Four and twenty blackbirds baked in a _____ie.

_____

_____

_____

cl, n, or r **3.** There came a little blackbird and nipped off her _____ose.

_____

_____

_____

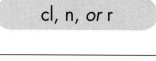 **4.** She whipped them all soundly and put them to _____ed.

_____

_____

_____

b, f, or r

f, sh, or str **5.** And Tom went crying down the _____eet.

_____

_____

_____

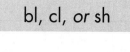 **6.** The mouse ran up the _____ock.

bl, cl, or sh

_____

_____

_____

d, p, or fl	**7.** Three, four, shut the _____oor.
	_____
	_____

kn, thr, or b	**8.** And he called for his fiddlers _____ee.
	_____
	_____

c, pl, or l	**9.** And one for the little boy that lives in the _____ane.
	_____
	_____

dr, pl, or g	**10.** He stuck in his thumb and pulled out a _____um.
	_____
	_____

3 Which Word Does Not Fit? Use the first word as a guide word to help you choose the word in the line that does not fit. Note how the first one has been done.

1. country: California   Egypt   France   United States   _**California**_

2. summer: beach   snow   sunshine   tans   _____

3. month: January   March   May   spring   _____

4. time: hour   minute   pound   second   _____

5. sea: beach   car   boat   swim   _____

6. trees: elm   peach   leaves   pine   _____

7. liquids: ice   soup   water   wine   _____

8. drinks: beer   coffee   straw   tea   _____

9. body: air   chest   lungs   spleen   _____

10. clothes: blouse   jeans   vest   wool   _____

11. women: cowboys   ladies   queens   females   _____

12. job: doctor   miner   smoker   tailor   _____

13. water: beach   lake   pond   sea   _____

14. baseball: base   bat   bunt   punt   _____

4 Silent Letters. In each of these words, there is one letter that you do not hear. This is called a silent letter. Write the word on the line. Then draw a line through the silent letter. Note how the first one has been done.

1. knit   _Knit_ _____   **7.** wrist _____

2. breath _____   **8.** climb _____

3. fetch _____   **9.** meant _____

4. claim _____   **10.** heart _____

5. wrong _____   **11.** lamb _____

6. thumb _____   **12.** watch _____

5 Words That Sound the Same. Put the right word on each line.

read *and* red

1. Dick sat in his _____ armchair and _____ his book until his wife came home from the meeting.

sea *and* see

2. The people ran for the seats on the top deck, so they could _____ the _____ better.

weak *and* week

3. Jill was still so _____ that she took another _____ off from work to rest.

threw *and* through

4. Mack wanted to get _____ with his work as fast as he could so he really _____ himself into it.

bare *and* bear

5. When the hunters returned to camp, they knew that a _____ had been there because the food chest was _____.

way *and* weigh

6. "By the _____," said Eddie, "did you remember to _____ yourself today?"

brake *and* break

7. "It will _____ Nick's heart when he hears that one _____ on his brand-new bike does not work," said Jill.

cents *and* sense

8. "It makes no _____ to spend seventy-five _____ on a candy bar," said Louise.

Say these words out loud. (A few of the words are new, but if you use the rules you have learned, you will have no trouble with them.)

shave	share	dare	dart	chart	cheek
such	Dutch	ditch	switch	swipe	pipe
claw	thaw	thin	grin	grow	flow
paint	pint	point	joint	join	coin
swell	smell	smile	while	wheat	heat
drove	stove	starve	carve	cart	smart

ail	bail	jail	pail	sail	
clap	lap	map	snap	trap	
beep	creep	jeep	sleep	sheep	
beach	bleach	peach	reach	teach	
dim	him	Jim	slim	trim	
book	look	took	shook	crooked	
boil	coil	oil	soil	spoil	
bunch	crunch	hunch	lunch	punch	
suck	stuck	stick	brick	bring	king

1 Choosing the Answer. Choose the right word, and fill it in on the line.

1. Tom was sleeping so _____ that he didn't hear the noise from the party next door.

 a. deadly   b. hardly   c. soundly   d. surely

2. Even _____ Mary had enough money to buy the dress, she decided not to get it after all.

 a. though   b. thought   c. through   d. threw

3. The boy pulled the door open and _____ into the refrigerator.

 a. piped   b. poured   c. peered   d. peeled

4. After Jim fed the baby, he patted her back to help her _____.

 a. burn   b. burp   c. burst   d. bust

5. Bob ate a half dozen, or _____, candy bars!

 a. sin   b. sip   c. sit   d. six

6. The _____ reason that Joan didn't do the dishes right away was that she wanted to watch the six o'clock news.

 a. maid   b. mail   c. main   d. many

7. "If you tell my wife what I bought her for her birthday, you will _____ all my fun," said Nick.

 a. soil   b. spell   c. spill   d. spoil

8. Mary didn't know the answer to the teacher's question, but she took a wild _____ anyway.

 a. guess   b. guest   c. guide   d. guilt

9. She had a _____ that it was the wrong answer.

 a. bunch   b. hunch   c. lunch   d. punch

2 Words That Mean the Same. Match each word below with the word that means the same.

brake	dirt	glitter	melt	shut	spoil
break	during	guide	rhyme	slim	tease

_____ **1.** close

_____ **2.** gleam

_____ **3.** kid

_____ **4.** lead

_____ **5.** rot

_____ **6.** shatter

_____ **7.** soil

_____ **8.** stop

_____ **9.** thaw

_____ **10.** thin

_____ **11.** verse

_____ **12.** while

3 Word Opposites. Match each word below with the word that means the opposite.

against	crooked	evening	lie	rare	thaw
cloudy	dirty	forgot	neat	sink	weak

_____ **1.** clean

_____ **2.** clear

_____ **3.** common

_____ **4.** float

_____ **5.** for

_____ **6.** freeze

_____ **7.** morning

_____ **8.** messy

_____ **9.** remembered

_____ **10.** straight

_____ **11.** strong

_____ **12.** truth

Word Index: Lessons 1-10

A
against
alphabet
Anne
armchair

B
babysit
bail
ban
basket
BC
beach
bee
beeswax
bend
berry
between
Bible
bigwig
billion
bird
blackbird
blink
blob
bloodstream
blouse
blown
blueberry
bluff
body
boot
Boston
bought
brand
brand-new
break
breathe
brick
bring
build
built
bunch
burp
bust

C
California
Canada
Canadian
catbird
catfish
cave
cereal
chain

change
cheek
chicken
children
chocolate
choke
claim
claw
cloud
cloudy
coil
coin
common
compound
copy
cornflakes
country
cover
cowboy
craps
creep
crooked
crunch

D
dart
dash
deadly
describe
diddle
dim
doctor
dollar
Donna
dozen
drank
draw
drew
dust
dusty
dwarves

E
early
eggshell
Egypt
eighty
either
El Dorado
elm
England
English
every
everywhere
example

F
fear
feeling
fiddle
fiddler
float
football
forefeet
forgot
form
forty-niner
fought
frame
France
fruit
fruitcake

G
gallon
gang
glitter
God
goes
goose
grain
grand
grandstand
grapefruit
grave
graveyard
grew
Griffiths
grin
grow
grown
grown-up
guide

H
half
heard
he's
hey
hidden
hold
host
human
hunch
hundred

I
important
instead
isn't
its

J
January
Japan
Jill
Jim
John

K
kept
kill
king
King Solomon
kneel
knit

L
lady
lapdog
Las Vegas
letter
lice
lifetime
liquid
lonely
lord
lover

M
maker
map
March
mass
May
meaning
meant
mention
meow
microwave
miner
mirror
mouth
move
munch

N
news
nip
noise

O

P
pail
paper

peach
pepperoni
person
Pinocchio
pint
pipe
pizza
point
post
potato
pouch
pound
proof
puff
punch
purr

Q
quart
queen

R
rail
rainbow
raise
react
reading
reason
record
refill
refrigerator
relate
remember
renew
rhyme
round

S
sail
sauce
saying
scribe
sea
sense
sentence
September
seventh
seventy
Seven Up
shack
share
sharp
shatter
shave
sheep

sheet
shell
ship
shoot
shore
shortstop
shower
shrill
sideways
silent
sin
slack
slang
slim
snack
snap
snob
Snow White
soil
somebody
someone
sometimes
soundly
soup
speaker
spell
spice
spin
spoil
spoke
sport
spray
spread
squid
stamp
stand
state
steam
stick
stink
stone
stove
strawberry
stuck
sugar
sunlight
sunshine
surely
Sutter, J.
swell
swipe

T
tailor
teabag
teach

team
tease
teaspoon
temple
tend
term
thaw
though
thousand
throne
tiny
tip
tomato
ton
touch
touchdown
towel
trap
trick
trim
trouble
troublemaker
truth

U
ugly
under
United States

V
vegetable
vowel

W
wall
warm
weak
weigh
well-known
whatever
wherever
wolves
wool
world
worth
written

X

Y
yolk

Z

Words for Study

sleepy	fourth	winter	mow
yawn	log	lawn	chessboard
asleep	awful	pawns	chess
become	dawn	crack	choice
breathing	lawful	fins	sister

LESSON 11
Sleeping

On most nights, as you start to get sleepy, you may yawn a few times. Yawning is a very common way for your body to draw in more air.

After you go to bed, changes start to happen in your body even before you fall asleep. Your body heat goes down, and your brain waves become more even. When you do fall asleep, your heart rate slows down, your body relaxes, and your breathing becomes very even.

Doctors say that we move through four stages of sleep each night. Each stage brings us into a more deep sleep. On most nights, we go through these stages four or five times.

Most dreaming takes place during the fourth stage, which is called REM. REM sleep lasts from five to twenty minutes at a time. During REM sleep, your eyes move around very quickly, but your arms and legs can't move at all. In fact, if anybody tried to wake you up, you would not be able to move for quite a few seconds.

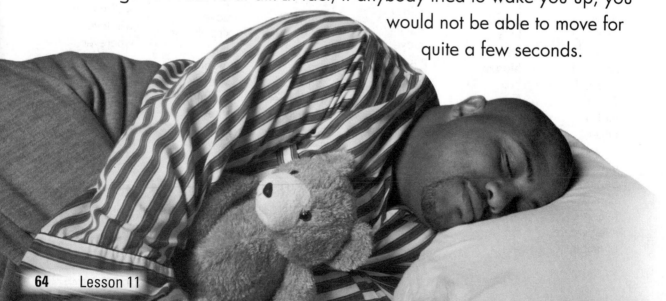

Nobody ever really sleeps "like a log." We move in our sleep as many as twenty to forty-five times every night. Much of this turning and moving happens when our bodies are going from one stage of sleep into the next. If we did not move at all during the time that we sleep, we could become very sick.

1 About the Reading. Answer these questions.

1. Why do we yawn when we are sleepy?

_____

2. List two changes that happen in the body before someone falls asleep.

a. _____

b. _____

3. List three changes that happen in the body after someone falls asleep.

a. _____

b. _____

c. _____

4. During what stage does most dreaming happen?

_____

5. What would you do if somebody woke you up during this stage?

_____

6. What would happen to your body if you did sleep like a log?

_____

What do you think?

7. Why do you think people dream?

_____

8. Do you remember most of your dreams, or do you forget them as soon as you wake up? _____

2 Word Sounds. Here are some words with *aw* in them. Use the words below to fill in the lines with the right answers. Note how the first one has been done.

awful	dawn	law	lawn	✓paws	thaws
claws	jaw	lawful	pawns	straw	yawn

1. People have hands; dogs have __*paws*_____.

Fish have fins; birds have _____.

2. In the winter it freezes; in spring, the ice _____.

You eat meat with a fork and sip Coke through a _____.

3. Last night, the boxer broke his _____.

As a rule, fighting's against the _____.

4. The lady got up at the crack of _____.

She raked the leaves and mowed the _____.

5. The second row on a chessboard is lined with _____.

If you're bored with chess, you tend to _____.

6. Smoking in lobbies is often not _____.

I hope you don't think this work is too _____.

3 Long and Short Vowels. Put the right words on the lines.

breath breathe	**1.** John's jacket was so tight that he could hardly _____. Sue had been running so hard that she had trouble catching her _____.
bath bathe	**2.** Mr. White always took a shower in the morning, but his wife liked to _____ just before dinner. The king took his _____ in a tub made of gold.
tap tape	**3.** Do you ever _____ your foot when you feel upset? Min-hee couldn't remember where she left the roll of _____.
scrap scrape	**4.** Ben threw his dog a _____ of ham that was left over from breakfast. It took Joan all afternoon to _____ the paint off the ceiling.
grip gripe	**5.** Andy liked to _____ about taxes even though he had no choice but to pay them. When Dave lost his _____ on the rope, he fell into the water.
twin twine	**6.** Ann had not seen her _____ sister since she moved to California. The cat got her paw twisted up in the ball of _____.

4 Putting Words in Order. Put the words in order so that each sentence makes sense.

1. White couldn't go Mr. sleep to

_____

2. counting first he sheep tried

_____

3. a cup fixed he himself of tea then

_____

4. asleep couldn't fall he still

_____

5. day fired for he job next on sleeping the the was

_____

Words for Study

honeybees	pollen	percent	chemicals
honey	groups	gone	hive
plant	colony	experts	stinger
flowers	beekeepers	disease	yellow

LESSON 12
Honeybees

Bees have been here for over 100 million years. There are about 20,000 kinds of bees, but only nine kinds of bees make honey. Honeybees are a big part of farming today. They are worth $15 billion each year in the United States alone. How? Bees help fruit to grow. Bees move from plant to plant looking for food that is in the plant's flowers. Pollen also sits in the flowers. It sticks to the bee's legs. When the bee moves to another flower, the pollens can mix. When bees carry pollen from one fruit tree flower to another, fruit begins to form.

Bees also make honey and beeswax. These are worth another $150 million each year just in the United States.

Honeybees live in groups. The groups are called colonies. One colony can be around 50,000 bees.

But something is happening. In late 2006, lots of bee colonies in the United States began to die. Some beekeepers lost 50 to 90 percent of their bees. Colonies can die very quickly, sometimes in a few weeks. What happens? The bees are just gone. And there are no dead bees. Honey and food are all that is left.

Why does this happen? Experts don't know yet. Some think it is pests or disease. Others say it is what the bees eat. It can be chemicals used by beekeepers or farmers. Some experts say it is a mix of these and other problems.

What can happen if this isn't stopped? Experts say not all honeybees will be wiped out. But food prices could jump or some foods could be harder to get.

1 About the Reading. Answer these questions.

1. How long have bees been around? _____

2. How many kinds of bees are there? _____

3. How many kinds of bees make honey? _____

4. How much are bees worth to United States farming each year?

_____

5. How do bees help fruit to form? _____

_____

_____

6. What things do bees make that are worth $150 million each year ?

_____

7. What are the groups called that honeybees live in? _____

8. What began happening in late 2006? _____

9. How quickly can a bee colony die? _____

10. What is one thing experts think could be the cause? _____

11. Do experts think all honeybees will die? _____

12. Why would food cost more or be harder to get if more bees die?

_____

2 Word Sounds. Choose the right word, and fill it in on the line.

smiles
miles
piles

1. A honeybee can fly about 15 _____ per hour.

five
hive
dive

2. Bees have _____ eyes.

tie
lie
die

3. If a bee loses its stinger, it will _____.

pipes
stripes
wipes

4. The honeybee is yellow with brown _____.

flowers
powers
towers

5. Honeybees go to between 50 and 100 _____ on each trip.

sunny
runny
honey

6. It takes 12 honeybees to make one teaspoon of _____.

must
trust
dust

7. Honeybees _____ go to 2 million flowers to make one pound of honey.

more
store
tore

8. Honey has _____ calories than sugar!

hive
live
give

9. You should never _____ honey to a baby.

3 Words That End in -y. Add -y to these words. Study the examples before you begin.

1. sleep + y = _____ *sleepy* _____   **4.** sugar + y = _____

2. water + y = _____   **5.** creep + y = _____

3. stick + y = _____   **6.** worth + y = _____

1. sun + y = _____ *sunny* _____   **4.** kit + y = _____

2. snap + y = _____   **5.** bud + y = _____

3. pig + y = _____   **6.** fog + y = _____

1. spice + y = _____ *spicy* _____   **4.** sauce + y = _____

2. shine + y = _____   **5.** shake + y = _____

3. noise + y = _____   **6.** wave + y = _____

4 Words That End in -ly. Put the right words on the lines. Study the example before you begin.

| barely | calmly | lonely | ✓quickly | sharply |
| bravely | cheaply | nearly | simply | weekly |

1. I _____**quickly**_____ ran to see what had happened after I heard the loud noise.

2. _____, you can't be in two places at one time!

3. Jim turned the wheel too _____ and nearly crashed into another car.

4. He did not seem scared. Instead, he _____ pulled his car out of the way.

5. Those pants are too small. You can _____ zip them!

6. Mary smiled _____ when the doctor came in to give her a shot.

7. My mother always said two could live almost as _____ as one.

8. Mrs. White sometimes felt _____ after her good friend moved away.

9. I went for a walk in the snow and _____ slid on a patch of ice.

10. Dan gives Bob a paycheck _____.

5 Compound Words. Use a word from **List A**, and add a word from **List B** to it to make a compound word for each sentence. Study the example before you begin.

List A	List B
after	bee
bee	ever
✓bees	keepers
honey	noon
sea	sick
table	spoon
team	✓wax
when	work

1. Honey and _____ **beeswax** _____ are two things bees make.

2. I like to have a snack in the _____.

3. Min-hee was _____ the whole time we were on the ship.

4. I like a _____ of honey in my tea.

5. One _____ colony can have around 50,000 bees.

6. It takes _____ for bees to build a hive.

7. Some _____ have lost 50 to 90 percent of their bee colonies.

8. _____ I see a bee, I run the other way!

6 Changing the _f_ to _v._ Change the _f_ to _v_ and add _-s_ or _-es_ to make each word plural. Study how the first two have been done. Then do the same with the remaining words.

1. leaf ___ **leaves** ___

2. wife ___ **wives** ___

3. knife _____

4. wolf _____

5. dwarf_____

6. self _____

7. half _____

8. life _____

Words for Study

handwriting	factors	tomorrow	drag
employer	studies	doesn't	large
certain	slant	uphill	whose
police	up-and-down	bright	allow
upon	present	downhill	young

LESSON 13
Handwriting

Everything we do tells other people something about who we are. Some people think that our handwriting tells a lot about us. Sometimes people hire handwriting experts. For example, an employer might hire a handwriting expert to find out if a certain person would be the right one for a job. Sometimes the police call upon handwriting experts to work with them on certain cases.

There are at least sixteen factors that a handwriting expert looks at when he studies handwriting. One factor is the slant of the letters. An up-and-down slant shows that the writer lives in the present and is ruled by his head. A right slant shows that the writer lives for tomorrow and goes by rules that other people have made. A left slant shows that the writer lives in the past, doesn't always go by the rules, and tends to keep to himself.

A second factor in studying handwriting is how the writing line goes. If the writer's lines tend to go uphill, he is a person who looks on the bright side of things. If the writing line goes downhill, the person is often sad and thinks life is a drag.

A third factor in studying handwriting is to note how big and wide the letters are. Large letters tell us that the person would really like to make something out of his life. Round letters show that the person can roll with the punches. Wide letters show a person who will let others see his feelings. However, letters that are not wide at all show a person who won't let others see who he really is.

1 About the Reading. Answer these questions.

1. List three of the main factors that a handwriting expert looks at when he studies handwriting.

a. _____

b. _____

c. _____

2. True or false? Read each sentence. If the sentence is true according to what you have just read, write *true* on the line to the left. If the sentence is false according to what you have just read, write *false* on the line to the left.

_____ **a.** A person who writes with an up-and-down slant lives for tomorrow.

_____ **b.** A person who slants his letters to the left lives in the past.

_____ **c.** A person whose writing line goes uphill looks on the bright side of things.

_____ **d.** A person whose writing line goes downhill looks on the bright side of things.

_____ **e.** Large letters show that the person can roll with the punches.

_____ **f.** A person whose letters are not wide at all does not let others see his feelings.

Just for Fun

3. Write your full name in the box.

```
┌──────────────────────────────────────────────┐
│                                              │
│                                              │
└──────────────────────────────────────────────┘
```

Study your handwriting and answer these questions according to what you have just read.

a. Do you think you live in the present, for tomorrow, or in the past?

_____

b. Do you think you look at the bright side of things, or do you think life is a drag?

_____

c. Do you think you would like to make something of your life?

_____

d. Do you think you let others see your feelings, or do you tend to hide them?

_____

What do you think?

4. Do you think handwriting experts can tell us something about who we really are?

_____

5. Based on your study of your own handwriting, would you want to change it, or do you like it just the way it is?

_____

2 Words That Mean the Same. Match each word below with the word that means the same.

allow	bright	double	marry	scream
barely	certain	large	present	shirt

_____ **1.** blouse

_____ **2.** big

_____ **3.** hardly

_____ **4.** let

_____ **5.** shiny

_____ **6.** sure

_____ **7.** today

_____ **8.** twice

_____ **9.** wed

_____ **10.** yell

3 Word Opposites. Match each word below with the word that means the opposite.

asleep	birth	summer	uphill	yesterday
begin	bright	sunny	won	young

_____ **1.** awake

_____ **2.** cloudy

_____ **3.** death

_____ **4.** downhill

_____ **5.** dull

_____ **6.** end

_____ **7.** lost

_____ **8.** old

_____ **9.** tomorrow

_____ **10.** winter

4 Vowel Sounds. Say the words below out loud. Then say the guide words out loud. Put the words under the guide words that have the same vowel sound. Study the example before you begin.

✓are	carve	fair	here	stare
bear	dear	hard	march	their
beer	deer	heart	peer	wear

Star	Air	Ear
1. _are_	1. _____	1. _____
2. _____	2. _____	2. _____
3. _____	3. _____	3. _____
4. _____	4. _____	4. _____
5. _____	5. _____	5. _____

Words for Study

tobacco	along	effects	nonsmoking
Americas	brought	medical	public
native	business	journal	Vermont
explorers	factory	Surgeon General	restaurant
Europe	health	cancer	army

LESSON 14
Smoking

People have been using tobacco for thousands of years. As early as 1000 BC people were chewing or smoking tobacco leaves. Tobacco first grew only in the Americas. It was used by the native peoples who lived there. But that all changed in the late 1400s when explorers from Europe reached the Americas. Along with fruit and other items, they were given tobacco as a gift by the natives.

By the mid-1500s, explorers had brought tobacco back to Europe. It became a huge hit. By 1600, tobacco was being farmed in the Americas. It was being grown and then sent back to England. There, tobacco had become a big business. In 1856, the first cigarette factory opened. It made cigarettes by rolling tobacco in paper. By 1900, cigarettes were a part of life. Men even bought jackets and hats made just for smoking.

But some people were starting to worry about the health effects of smoking. In 1858, doctors brought it up for the first time. It was written about in an English medical journal. In the 1950s, more doctors wrote about a tie between smoking and lung cancer. By the mid-1960s, many experts worried about the health risks of smoking.

In 1964, the Surgeon General wrote a report that said smoking causes cancer. By 1970, ads for cigarettes were being banned on television.

In 1973, the United States put into place its first smoking ban. The rule said all planes must have some nonsmoking seats. Stronger plane smoking bans were added in 1987 and 1990.

States began banning smoking in public places in 1993. Vermont was the first state to do so. In 2010, 26 states banned smoking at work, in restaurants, and in bars. Today all 50 states have some kind of smoking ban in place. Even the United States Army bans smoking. That ban went into effect in 2008.

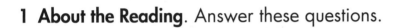

1 About the Reading. Answer these questions.

  1. When did people first start using tobacco? _____

  2. Where did it begin growing? _____

  3. How did people first use tobacco leaves? _____

  4. When did explorers to the Americas try tobacco? _____

  5. When did explorers bring tobacco back to Europe? _____

  6. In what year did the first cigarette factory open? _____

  7. How did it make cigarettes? _____

  8. By 1970, what was being banned from television? _____

What do you think?

  9. Do you think today's smoking bans are too strict? Why or why not?

_____

_____

  10. What are some things people can do to stop smoking?

_____

_____

2 True or False? Read each sentence. If the sentence is true according to the time line, write *true* on the line to the left. If the sentence is false according to the time line, write *false* on the line to the left.

_____ **1.** Tobacco is smoked in Europe in 6000 BC.

_____ **2.** Explorers bring tobacco back to England in the 1500s.

_____ **3.** The first cigarette factory opens in the Americas in 1856.

_____ **4.** The Surgeon General says smoking causes cancer.

_____ **5.** Every state has smoking bans.

_____ **6.** In 1973, the United States bans smoking in cars.

_____ **7.** The first state to ban smoking is California.

_____ **8.** The United States Army has a ban on smoking.

3 Working with Words That Rhyme. Say the words at the left out loud. Then put each word on the right line so the sentences make sense.

more
door
pour
for

1. First, I opened the refrigerator _____. Then I looked _____ the milk. I needed to _____ another glass for my daughter. She wanted _____ to drink.

best
test
rest
nest

2. There was no time to _____! The small bird had fallen out of his _____. He had tried his _____ to _____ his wings.

beat street seat meet	**3.** I was driving down the _____ to _____ my friend Mark. All at once, I was thrown from my _____. I was in a crash! Someone had tried to _____ the red light.

tie try dry sky	**4.** The _____ looked clear. There was no rain in sight. It looked _____ outside. I thought I would _____ taking a walk. I bent to _____ my shoes.

bent tent rent went	**5.** The pole for the _____ was so _____ that Mary _____ over to her friend's store to see if she could _____ a better one for the camping trip.

4 Words That End in *-er*. Add *-er* to these words. Study the examples before you begin.

1. stick + er = __sticker__

4. crack + er = _____

2. hang + er = _____

5. mow + er = _____

3. heat + er = _____

1. smoke + er = __smoker__

4. dance + er = _____

2. drive + er = _____

5. freeze + er = _____

3. make + er = _____

1. trap + er = __trapper__

4. zip + er = _____

2. bat + er = _____

5. swim + er = _____

3. knit + er = _____

Words for Study

hobby	barbed	says	fence
brink	reported	hooked	field
necktie	sold	link	cutters
snagged	gold-plated	strand	utter
above	swizzle	helicopter	crook

L E S S O N   1 5
A Very Strange Hobby

Have you ever heard any of these names: Hold Fast, Saw Tooth, Wrap Around, Brink Twist, or Necktie? If not, then you haven't been snagged by one of the strangest hobbies in the United States. All of the names listed above are kinds of barbed wire that have been made in the United States since 1867.

What do you do with barbed wire after you get it? Well, one man is reported to have sold 4,000 gold-plated, barbed-wire swizzle sticks to a big store. At last report, every one of these swizzle sticks had been snapped up for eight dollars a set.

Not all people sell their barbed wire. As one barbed wire fan says, "I'm hooked on barbed wire because it's a link to this country's past. Barbed wire is one of the things that won the West."

The main goal of people who love barbed wire is to own at least one strand of every kind of barbed wire ever made. However, this can't be done because some kinds of barbed wire are no longer around.

After all, how could people living in 1867 have known that the people living today would be so crazy about barbed wire? Strands of barbed wire that are very rare have sold for as much as thirty to forty dollars a strand.

One man, who is a doctor, is so stuck on barbed wire that he hunts for old barbed wire by helicopter. In his spare time, he spends hours flying over miles of fences that are no longer used. Whenever he sights something that looks good, he sets his helicopter down in a field, takes out a pair of wire cutters and snags off a strand or two of barbed wire.

1 About the Reading. Answer these questions.

1. List three brand names of barbed wire.

2. Describe how one man made a lot of money with his barbed wire.

_____

3. What is the main goal of barbed-wire fans? _____

_____

4. The kinds of barbed wire were most likely named for

_____

    a. the people who first made them.

    b. the way they looked.

    c. the town where they were first made.

    d. the way they were used.

5. Put what the doctor does in looking for barbed wire in the right order.

> He flies over miles of fence looking for barbed wire.
>
> He sets his helicopter down in a field.
>
> He sees something that looks good.
>
> He takes out his wire cutters and cuts off a strand.
>
> The doctor gets into his helicopter.

a. _____

b. _____

c. _____

d. _____

e. _____

What do you think?

6. The people who most likely used barbed wire in 1867 were _____

   a. doctors.   b. farmers.   c. cattlemen.   d. outlaws.

7. Why did these people use it? _____

_____

2 Working with Words That Rhyme. Say the words at the left out loud. Then put each word on the right line so the sentences make sense.

cold
folded
gold
sold
	1. It was too _____ to look for _____, so
	   the men _____ up their tents, _____
	   their tools, and headed south.

brink
drink
sink
stink

2. Whenever Ms. Parks had a bad cold, she felt she was at the

_____ of death. As she got a _____

of water from the _____, she could tell that pile of

dishes was beginning to _____.

brand
land
strand
grand

3. Billy thought it was _____ that he found a

new _____ of barbed wire on the farmer's

_____. It was a _____ that he had not

seen before!

lacked
Mack
rack
sack

4. _____ wanted to buy all the chocolate candy

bars on the _____, but he _____ a

_____ to carry them all home in.

bare
cared
share
spare

5. Mr. White's wife _____ a lot about other people

and wanted to _____ what she had, but her

own house was so _____ that she wasn't able to

_____ very much.

butter
cutters
Sutter
utter

6. Mr. _____ didn't _____ a word

when his crazy wife used wire _____ to spread

_____ on her toast.

luck
stuck
sucked
tucked

7. After Jill _____ the baby in her crib, the

baby _____ her thumb into her mouth,

_____ it for a few minutes, and fell fast asleep.

"What good _____!" thought Jill.

bring
king
sing
sting

8. The _____ asked his lord to _____

something for his bee _____ and then

_____ him a song to calm his nerves.

griped
ripe
swiped
wiped

9. As Mr. Lane _____ the table, he

_____ to the diner that somebody had

_____ all the _____ peaches from

the box in the back room.

book
crook
hook
look

10. When the _____ gave the policeman a mean

_____, the policeman said, "You're not going to

get off the _____, Bud. We're going to throw the

_____ at you."

3 How Do You Say It? Choose the right word below, and write it on the line. Study
the example before you begin.

bar	bunch	✓flock	loaf	pot
book	can	herd	pack	quart
box	deck	load	pair	school

1. a _____**flock**_____ of birds

2. a _____ of bread

3. a _____ of cards

4. a _____ of cereal

5. a _____ of cigarettes

6. a _____ of coffee

7. a _____ of cows

8. a _____ of fish

9. a _____ of grapes

10. a _____ of milk

11. a _____ of pants

12. a _____ of peas

13. a _____ of soap

14. a _____ of stories

15. a _____ of wash

Review: Lessons 1-15

Say these words out loud. (A few of the words are new, but if you use the rules you have learned, you will have no trouble with them.)

plain	rain	Spain	sprain	stain
ash	cash	dash	flash	trash
bleed	deed	greed	seed	weed
click	kick	stick	tick	trick
bold	cold	fold	sold	told
couch	crouch	grouch	ouch	pouch
blue	clue	due	glue	Sue
bust	crust	dust	must	rust
caught	fought	thought	bought	brought

1 Choosing the Answer. Choose the right word, and put it on the line.

1. Glue can make your hands very _____.
   a. shiny   b. snappy   c. sorry   d. sticky

2. Everybody liked Louise's pies because her crusts were so _____.
   a. bouncy   b. flaky   c. sticky   d. watery

3. When it is very _____, drivers can see better using their dim lights instead of their bright lights.
   a. clear   b. cloudy   c. foggy   d. sunny

4. Ms. Bond _____ her car loan in three years.
   a. recorded   b. refunded   c. repaid   d. reported

5. It took the woman a long time to find the folder because she had _____ it in the wrong place.
   a. filed   b. filled   c. filmed   d. firmed

6. When a black cat _____ your path, do you feel you're going to have bad luck?
   a. bosses   b. crosses   c. losses   d. tosses

7. Joan was all dressed up and had _____ to go.
   a. nobody   b. no one   c. nothing   d. nowhere

8. Many people are _____ in the morning until they have had a cup of coffee.
   a. couches   b. crouches   c. grouches   d. pouches

9. Kate added two cups of nuts to the cake _____ before she poured it into the baking pan.
   a. batter   b. better   c. bitter   d. butter

10. At the sale, the duke _____ three thousand dollars on the painting of the English queen.

    a. bad   b. bed   c. bid   d. bud

11. Joan bought a jar of honey for herself and a jar of _____ jam for her aunt.

    a. grape   b. grip   c. gripe   d. group

12. Knitting is my _____. It helps me to relax.

    a. hobby   b. lobby   c. baby   d. job

13. The _____ is the day this country celebrates claiming its freedom from England.

    a. Christmas   b. birthday   c. Fourth of July   d. New Year's Day

14. The War Between the States was between the _____.

    a. employers and the workers   c. North and the South

    b. East and the West   d. English and the Canadians

2 Silent Letters. In each of these words, there are one or two silent letters. Write each word on the line. Then draw a line through the silent letters. Study the example before you begin.

1. wrote ~~wrote~~

2. dumb _____

3. badge _____

4. Dutch _____

5. young _____

6. build _____

7. knee _____

8. dodge _____

9. batch _____

10. writer _____

11. witch _____

12. certain _____

3 Matching. Choose the right word below for each sentence.

alphabet	mower	pepper	rainbow	towel
fence	oven	piggy	stamp	wax

1. If you want a pot of gold, look for the end of the _____.

2. If you want to bake cupcakes, use an _____.

3. If you want to cut the grass, use a lawn _____.

4. If you want to dry your hands, use a _____.

5. If your want to keep others out of your yard, build a _____.

6. If you want to mail a letter, you need a _____.

7. If you want to find numbers in the phone book, learn the _____.

8. If you want to save your change, put your coins in a _____ bank.

9. If you want your floors to be shiny, use some floor _____.

10. If you want your food to taste spicy, use more _____.

4 Word Sounds. Say the words in each line out loud. Find the word in which the underlined letter or letters do not make the same sound as they do in the other words. Write the odd word on the line to the right. Study the example before you begin.

1. h<u>o</u>se	n<u>o</u>se	r<u>o</u>se	wh<u>o</u>se	*whose*
2. <u>c</u>ave	<u>c</u>ertain	<u>c</u>ode	<u>c</u>ousin	_____
3. all<u>ow</u>	gr<u>ow</u>	m<u>ow</u>	rainb<u>ow</u>	_____
4. b<u>a</u>th	b<u>a</u>the	scr<u>a</u>pe	t<u>a</u>pe	_____
5. c<u>ou</u>nt	<u>ou</u>ch	s<u>ou</u>nd	s<u>ou</u>p	_____
6. ch<u>ea</u>ply	h<u>ea</u>ding	h<u>ea</u>ter	w<u>ea</u>k	_____
7. <u>g</u>inger	<u>g</u>ood	<u>g</u>oose	<u>g</u>uide	_____

5 Compound Words. Use a word from **List A**, and add a word from **List B** to it to make a compound word for each sentence. Study the example before you begin.

List A	List B
ash	body
baby	cake
busy	coach
cheese	crackers
fire	glasses
✓lip	line
police	sitter
stage	✓stick
sun	tray
under	woman

1. If a woman wants her lips to look red, she uses ___lipstick___ .

2. If you want to go out for the evening, hire a _____ to look after your children.

3. If the sun is too bright for your eyes, wear _____ .

4. If a smoker needs something for his ashes, he uses an _____ .

5. If you want to make lots of noise on the Fourth of July, get some _____ .

6. If you need to tell someone about a crime that you saw, you can talk to a _____ .

7. When people went from city to city in the West a long time ago, they rode on a _____ .

8. If you care about how much you weigh, stay away from _____ .

9. If you want to remember an important rule in your notebook, _____ it.

10. If you want to know everything that's happening on your block, ask a _____ .

Word Index: Lessons 1–15

A

above
against
allow
along
alphabet
America
Ann(e)
armchair
army
ash
ashtray
asleep
awful

B

babysit
babysitter
bail
ban
barbed
barely
basket
bathe
batter
BC
beach
become
bee
beekeeper
beeswax
bend
berry
between
Bible
bigwig
billion
bird
bitter
blackbird
blink
blob
bloodstream
blouse
blown

blueberry
bluff
body
bold
boot
boss
Boston
bought
bouncy
boxer
brand
brand-new
bravely
break
breathe
breathing
brick
bright
bring
brink
brought
buddy
build
built
bunch
burp
business
bust
busy
busybody

C

California
Canada
Canadian
cancer
catbird
catfish
cattlemen
cave
cereal
certain
chain
change
cheaply
cheek

cheesecake
chemical
chess
chessboard
chicken
children
chocolate
choice
choke
claim
claw
click
cloud
cloudy
clue
coil
coin
colony
common
compound
copy
cornflakes
couch
country
cover
cowboy
crack
cracker
craps
creep
creepy
crook
crooked
crouch
crunch
crust
cutters

D

dancer
dart
dash
dawn
deadly
deed
describe

diddle
dim
disease
doctor
doesn't
dollar
Donna
double
downhill
dozen
drag
drank
draw
drew
driver
drunk
dust
dusty
dwarf

E

early
effect
eggshell
Egypt
eighty
either
El Dorado
elm
employer
England
English
Europe
every
everywhere
example
expert
explorer

F

factor
factory
fear
feeling
fence

fiddle
fiddler
field
fin
firecracker
flaky
flash
float
flood
flower
foggy
fold
folder
football
forefeet
forgot
form
forty-niner
fought
fourth
Fourth of July
frame
France
freedom
freezer
fruit
fruitcake

G

gallon
gang
glitter
God
goes
gold-plated
gone
goose
grain
grand
grandstand
grapefruit
grave
graveyard
greed
grew
Griffiths

grin
grip
gripe
grouch
group
grow
grown
grown-up
guide

H

half
handwriting
hanger
health
heard
heater
helicopter
he's
hey
hidden
hive
hobby
hold
honey
honeybee
hook
host
human
hunch
hundred

I

important
instead
isn't
its

J

January
Japan
Jill
Jim
John
journal

July

K

kept
kill
king
King Solomon
kitty
kneel
knit
knitter

L

lady
lapdog
large
Las Vegas
lawful
lawn
letter
lice
lifetime
link
lipstick
liquid
log
lonely
lord
lover

M

maker
map
March
mass
May
meaning
meant
medical
mention
meow
microwave
miner
mirror
mouth

move
mow
mower
munch

N

native
nearly
necktie
nest
news
New Year's
   Day
nip
noise
noisy
nonsmoking
no one
nowhere

O

order
ouch

P

pail
paper
pawn
peach
pepperoni
percent
person
piggy
Pinocchio
pint
pipe
pizza
plant
point
police
policeman
policewoman
pollen
post
potato

pouch
pound
power
present
proof
public
puff
punch
purr

Q

quart
queen

R

rail
rainbow
raise
react
reading
reason
record
refill
refrigerator
relate
remember
renew
report
restaurant
rhyme
round
runny
rust

S

sail
sauce
saucy
saying
says
scrap
scrape
scribe
sea
seasick

sense
sentence
September
seventh
seventy
Seven Up
shack
shaky
share
sharp
sharply
shatter
shave
sheep
sheet
shell
ship
shoot
shore
shortstop
shot
shower
shrill
sideways
silent
simply
sin
sister
sitter
slack
slang
slant
sleepy
slim
smoker
snack
snag
snap
snappy
snob
Snow White
soil
sold
somebody
someone
sometimes

soundly
soup
Spain
speaker
spell
spice
spicy
spin
spoil
spoke
sport
spray
spread
squid
stagecoach
stamp
stand
state
steam
stick
sticker
sticky
sting
stinger
stink
stone
stove
strand
strawberry
stripe
stuck
study
suck
sugar
sugary
sunglasses
sunlight
sunshine
surely
Surgeon
   General
Sutter, J.
swell
swimmer
swipe
swizzle

T

table
tablespoon
tailor
tape
teabag
teach
team
teamwork
tease
teaspoon
temple
tend
term
thaw
though
thousand
throne
tiny
tip
tobacco
tomato
tomorrow
ton
toss
touch
touchdown
towel
tower
trap
trapper
trash
trick
trim
trouble
troublemaker
truth
tuck
twine

U

ugly
under
underline
United States

up-and-down
uphill
upon
utter

V

vegetable
Vermont
vowel

W

wall
war
warm
wash
watery
wavy
wax
weak
weigh
well-known
we're
whatever
whenever
wherever
whose
winter
wolf
wool
world
worth
worthy
written

X

Y

yard
yawn
yellow
yolk
young

Z

zipper

Words for Study

basketball	mammals	protect	calves
heavily	products	beluga	threat
efforts	endangered	Alaskan	action
ocean	species	future	pollution

LESSON 16
Whales

There are more than forty kinds of whales in the world. Many whales are quite large. The blue whale may be the largest of all animals. It can grow as long as 100 feet. That's about as long as a basketball court. Blue whales can weigh up to 160 tons.

Whales were hunted heavily in the 1800s. Most were hunted for their oil and bones. Many whales were hunted until there were almost none left.

But efforts began in 1946 to save whales. Some countries formed a group to help cut back whale hunting. Then in 1972 the United States passed a strict act. It banned hunting ocean mammals in United States waters. It also banned products made from whales from coming into the country.

In 1973 the United States passed the Endangered Species Act. This act works to protect certain plants and animals. It lists plants and animals that are becoming rare and need protection.

Thirteen kinds of whales found in United States waters are on the Endangered Species List. Another whale was added to the list in 2008. It is a kind of beluga whale found in Alaskan waters.

Beluga whales are one of the smallest kinds of whales. They are between 13 and 20 feet long. They weigh between 2,000 and 3,000 pounds.

What will happen to these endangered whales? The future isn't known for some. Most larger whales have few calves. They only have one every two to four years. It may take many years for these whales to come back.

And there are still threats to whales today. Some threats are due to human actions like pollution, boats, and noise.

But some whales have come back. The California gray whale is one such whale. The gray whale had been protected since 1946. Twice there were almost none left. But they came back. Now there are about 22,000. In 1994 the California gray whale was taken off the Endangered Species List.

1 About the Reading. Answer these questions.

1. How many kinds of whales are there? _____

2. Which whale may be the largest animal in the world? _____

3. How long can it grow? _____

4. When were whales hunted heavily? _____

5. What did the act passed in 1972 ban?

    a. _____

    b. _____

6. What does the Endangered Species Act do? _____

_____

7. How many kinds of whales found in United States waters are on the
Endangered Species List? _____

8. What kind of whale was added to the list in 2008? _____

9. Where is it found? _____

10. List two threats to whales due to human actions. _____

_____

11. Which whale has come back? _____

12. How many of them are there? _____

13. When was it taken off the Endangered Species List? _____

What do you think?

14. What do you think should be done when an animal species is endangered?

_____

_____

2 True or False? Read each sentence. Write *true* on the line to the left if the sentence
is true. Write *false* on the line to the left if the sentence is false.

_____ **1.** Whales were hunted heavily in the 1800s.

_____ **2.** Most whales were hunted for food.

_____ **3.** Some countries formed a group to grow whale hunting.

_____ **4.** In 1972, the United States passed a strict act to ban
whale hunting around the world.

_____ **5.** In 1903, the United States passed the Endangered Species Act.

_____ **6.** The beluga whale is one of the smallest kinds of whales.

_____ **7.** Beluga whales weigh between 2,000 and 3,000 tons.

_____ **8.** Most large whales have few calves.

_____ **9.** Human actions such as pollution, boats, and noise are still threats to whales today.

_____ **10.** The blue whale was taken off the Endangered Species List in 1994.

3 Putting Words in Order. Put the words in order so that each sentence makes sense.

1. saw   Canada   in   whale   I   once   a

_____

2. Sue   friends   her   had   a   breakfast   her   birthday   with   on

_____

3. bike   ride   took   Becky   Friday   a   on

_____

4. basketball   Andy   his   plays   with   dad

_____

5. A   arm   bug   bit   on   Tuesday   my

_____

4 Changing the -y to -i. Study how the first set has been done. Then do the same with the remaining words.

1. bumpy   _bumpier_   _bumpiest_

2. dirty   _____   _____

3. easy   _____   _____

4. friendly   _____   _____

5. funny   _____   _____

6. happy   _____   _____

7. needy   _____   _____

8. guilty   _____   _____

9. muddy   _____   _____

10. healthy   _____   _____

5 More Work with Changing the -y to -i. Say the words below out loud. Then put them on the right lines.

easily	fussily	happily	luckily	noisily	sleepily

1. After the king and queen were married, they lived _____ ever after.

2. The baby began to cry and _____ dropped the toy.

3. The children ran and played _____ at the birthday party.

4. Andy peered at the clock _____ and dozed off again.

5. _____, Roy didn't have to work on Wednesday so he could take his aunt to the doctor.

6. Some people can _____ make any food without using a cookbook.

6 Which Word Fits Best? For each sentence, choose the right answer from the four choices, and put it on the line.

1. Herd is to cows as mob is to _____.
   a. crowd   b. noise   c. people   d. street

2. Eel is to fish as whale is to _____.
   a. fish   b. mammal   c. school   d. swim

3. Forget is to remember as lose is to _____.
   a. find   b. keep   c. loss   d. mind

4. Hive is to bees as barn is to _____.
   a. hay   b. horses   c. rakes   d. ducks

5. Elm is to tree as rose is to _____.
   a. bud   b. flower   c. lovely   d. vase

6. Bunt is to baseball as punt is to _____.
   a. foot   b. football   c. fourth down   d. kick

7. Wool is to sheep as hide is to _____.
   a. cow   b. dog   c. pig   d. ram

8. Mirror is to glass as chairs are to _____.
   a. bricks   b. coal   c. glass   d. wood

9. Before is to after as yesterday is to _____.
   a. past   b. present   c. today   d. tomorrow

10. Always is to never as everywhere is to _____.
   a. no one   b. nowhere   c. everything   d. nothing

Bart	Charles	shotgun	poet
period	high-class	whirling	cause
robberies	middle-aged	sign	deserve
success	he'd	holdup	poem
struck	bushes	earn	empty

LESSON 17

Black Bart (1829–1917?)

Black Bart was better at holding up stagecoaches in the Old West than any other man. He robbed stagecoaches for more than eight years before he was caught. During this period he pulled off more than thirty robberies without ever firing a shot.

There were four main reasons for Black Bart's eight years of success. He always laid careful plans. He always worked alone. He never struck near home. He always kept his plans to himself.

Black Bart, whose real first name was Charles, got his start in crime in a strange way. He was a high-class, middle-aged teacher who loved to play jokes on people. One day he was riding along the road after school when he heard the stagecoach coming down the grade. He knew the driver and thought that, just for fun, he'd give him a scare.

Black Bart hid his horse in the bushes, tied a cloth over his face, and broke a stick from a bush to use as a gun. When the stagecoach came along, he stepped out into the road and told the driver to hold up. Nobody was riding shotgun on the stagecoach, and the driver looked very scared.

"Throw out the box!" roared Black Bart.

The driver pulled the box from under the seat and tossed it out. The box just happened to land on a rock. It broke open with such a crash that Bart jumped back off the road. The driver thought that this was his chance. He laid the whip to his horses, and the stagecoach went whirling away.

Black Bart

In the box was the real thing—about two thousand dollars. As Bart picked it up, he thought to himself, "If I can get as much in two minutes by playing a little joke like this as I can in two years of teaching school, maybe I had better quit teaching and stick to joking."

And that's just what he did. Every time he robbed a stagecoach, he would leave behind a verse or two and sign it Black Bart the PO8. This is why he's known as Black Bart to this day.

1 About the Reading. Answer these questions.

1. What was Black Bart's real first name? _____

2. For how many years was Black Bart a holdup man? _____

3. How many robberies did he pull off before he was caught? _____

4. How had Black Bart earned his living before he became a holdup man?

_____

5. About how much money did Black Bart make in his first holdup?

_____

6. Describe what Black Bart meant when he called his first holdup "a little joke."

_____

7. List four reasons why Black Bart was so good at holding up stagecoaches.

a. _____

b. _____

c. _____

d. _____

8. Based on what Black Bart says, how much money did teachers earn back then?

_____

What do you think?

9. Why do you think Black Bart signed his notes "the PO8"? _____

_____

10. Do you think it was wrong for Black Bart to rob stagecoaches?

_____

_____

2 Words That Mean the Same. Match the words below with the words that mean the same.

| alive | cause | earn | limbs | strip |
| all right | clue | high-class | robbery | verse |

_____ **1.** arms and legs   _____ **6.** okay

_____ **2.** deserve   _____ **7.** poem

_____ **3.** hint   _____ **8.** reason

_____ **4.** holdup   _____ **9.** rich

_____ **5.** living   _____ **10.** undress

3 Word Opposites. Match the words below with the words that mean the opposite.

awful	dozed	froze	harmful	scared
cool	fresh	full	leave	under

_____ 1. above

_____ 2. awoke

_____ 3. bold

_____ 4. empty

_____ 5. great

_____ 6. helpful

_____ 7. remain

_____ 8. stale

_____ 9. thawed

_____ 10. warm

4 A Verse from Black Bart. Here is an example of one of Black Bart's verses. See if you can put the words below on the right lines.

able	bread	curses	hung
blame	chance	dead	verses

This is my way to get money and _____.

When I have a _____, why should I refuse it?

I'll not need either when I'm _____,

And I only tax those who are _____ to lose it.

So _____ me not for what I've done,

I don't deserve your _____.

And if for some cause I must be _____.

Let it be for my _____.

5 The Ending -ful. Say the words below out loud. Then put them on the right lines, so the sentences make sense.

fearful	hopeful	mouthful	successful	truthful
forgetful	meaningful	spiteful	thoughtful	wasteful

1. The employer told the new workers that if they wanted to be _____, all they had to do was work hard.

2. Whenever Pinocchio wasn't _____, his nose grew.

3. Charles had a _____ of food and could not answer June's question right away.

4. When the teacher opened the Christmas gift from her second-grade class, she said, "Why, children, how _____ of you!"

5. Donna was so _____ of dogs that she wouldn't go to the park.

6. Mack wrote his wife a poem about their love for each other. It was very _____ to her.

7. Jack was so _____ that he put notes all over his house to remind himself about things he had to do.

8. The doctor was _____ that Mr. Long would be able to go back to work in one or two months.

9. Do you think it's _____ to spend money on clothes when you don't really need them?

10. A _____ person makes it his business to hurt other people's feelings.

Words for Study

Earth	rivers	natural	simple
April	senator	resources	forests
planet	Wisconsin	energy	reduce
environment	awareness	recycle	surprise
issue	Gaylord Nelson	celebrations	complex

LESSON 18
Earth Day

Earth Day falls on April 22. It is a day to learn about our planet and how to take care of it. The first Earth Day happened in 1970. At that time, the environment was not such a big issue. Laws that help protect the planet were not in place. Many cities were choked by air pollution. Rivers were dirty. But Earth Day helped to change all of that.

A senator from Wisconsin saw the need for action. He called on people to help raise awareness of environmental issues. His name was Gaylord Nelson. On April 22, 1970, twenty million people across America celebrated the first Earth Day. Now Earth Day is celebrated each year on April 22 around the world.

On Earth Day, people learn how to make choices that help keep our planet healthy. They learn of the dangers that face the environment. They learn how to protect natural resources like air and water. They learn how to do things around their homes to help save the planet. People can learn easy ways to use less water, save energy, and recycle.

Earth Day celebrations happen everywhere! They take place in towns, in businesses, and in schools. And there are lots of simple ways to join in. People can take part in group walks or help clean up parks. They

WE RECYCLE

can plant trees. Businesses can start recycling. Kids can learn tips and fun ways to help protect our planet.

Thanks to Earth Day, new laws were made to help protect the environment. Today, the air we breathe is getting cleaner. Our forests are being protected. And around the world, awareness of environmental issues is being raised.

But you don't have to wait for Earth Day to take care of our planet. You can do easy things each day to help protect the environment. You can buy products that reduce pollution and save energy. You can recycle. Every day can be Earth Day.

1 About the Reading. Answer these questions according to what you have just read.

1. When is Earth Day celebrated? _____

2. Why did Gaylord Nelson think we needed Earth Day? _____

_____

3. Where can Earth Day celebrations take place? _____

_____

What do you think?

4. Do you think it's important to reduce pollution and save energy? If yes, what do

you do? _____

_____

2 Word Sounds. Use the words at the left to fill in the answers.

sprained
sprawled
spray
sprinted

1. The young boy _____ for the house in the hope that he could get out of the way of the skunk's _____. However, he was running so fast that he tripped over the limb of an elm tree and was soon _____ on the ground. The doctor told him that he had _____ his wrist.

stranger
streets
strike
strong

2. The _____ was so _____ that everybody was very nice when they saw him on the _____ because they were scared he would _____ them.

swiftly
swimming
swinging
switch
swung

3. The fighter _____ so _____ that he caught the other boxer by surprise. His head was _____, and he knew he would have to _____ to another way of _____ just to stay in the fight.

scraped
screamed
screen
scrubbing

4. When Charles _____ his arm on the _____ door, he _____ so loudly that his wife stopped _____ the floor to go see what had happened.

squeezed
squirrel
squirt

5. The _____ _____ his way into the box, so the skunk couldn't _____ him.

struck
straight
strained
stroke

6. Will _____ to think of what to do for his son's birthday. At first he couldn't think _____. Then an idea _____ him! The amusement park! It was a _____ of luck that the park had just opened.

3 The Ending -less. Say the words below out loud. Then put them on the lines so the sentences make sense.

breathless	meatless	sleepless	thoughtless
cloudless	needless	sleeveless	useless
hairless	pointless	sugarless	worthless

1. It was so hot on Tuesday morning that May decided to wear a
   _____ dress to work.

2. Mark was running at a _____ pace through the whole course.

3. Min-hee hoped a warm glass of milk would put an end to this
   _____ night.

4. Ann worried about her teeth so she would only chew _____ gum.

5. Mack was so _____ that he refused to buy a Mother's Day card.

6. The man at the store told the miner that what he had in his sack was fool's gold,
   which was _____.

7. Mrs. Waters served _____ meals every Friday.

8. Tim looked at the _____ sky and knew it would be a good day
   for sailing.

9. The rusted knife was _____, so John threw it away.

10. Mrs. White thought it was _____ to celebrate her birthday since
    none of her friends were in town.

11. After he had his head shaved, Andy was shocked at his _____
    head in the mirror.

12. "_____ to say," said the teacher, "we will have homework to do
    for tomorrow's class."

4 Same or Opposite? Write *same* on the line to the left if the two words mean nearly the same thing. Write *opposite* if the two words are opposite in meaning. Study the example before you begin.

__*same*_____ **1.** burst *and* break

_____ **2.** cash *and* money

_____ **3.** future *and* past

_____ **4.** fresh *and* stale

_____ **5.** heavy *and* light

_____ **6.** damp *and* wet

_____ **7.** bathe *and* wash

_____ **8.** simple *and* complex

_____ **9.** soft *and* hard

_____ **10.** squeal *and* tell on

_____ **11.** summer *and* winter

_____ **12.** swipe *and* rob

_____ **13.** thick *and* thin

_____ **14.** brave *and* fearful

5 Spelling Check. The answers to the clues are listed at the left. As you can see, the letters of the words are all mixed up. Spell the words the right way on the lines to the right.

a c h M r

1. _____ This is the third month of the year.

p y e m t

2. _____ Your glass is either half full or half this.

t E r a h

3. _____ This is our planet.

k o r s t

4. _____ Some people think this brings babies.

a a J n r u y

5. _____ This is the first month of the year.

e e n r v

6. _____ Some people lose this when they get scared.

l a m m m a

7. _____ A whale is this kind of animal.

l i p t o l u n o

8. _____ I think everybody should help to reduce this.

a b i n o r w

9. _____ Some people think that a pot of gold is at the end of this.

e e e c h s

10. _____ This is what the rat takes in a well-known children's song.

Words for Study

galley	battle	flesh	port
inland	mainly	rise	whom
guard	convicts	push	trade
remove	hell	forward	temperature
wounded	below	thrown	there's

LESSON 19
Jails on the High Seas

Until the coming of steam, the galley was the fastest thing on the inland sea. Galleys were used to guard the coast and to remove ships that were wounded in battle. The galley was mainly an open boat for four hundred men. Who manned the oars that made the galley move so swiftly through the waters? Convicts.

Once a convict was sent to the galleys, he was no longer a man. He was an oar. He was stripped of all his clothes and put into a gang of five. Until the end of his days, he would eat, sleep, and work with the men in his gang. The men either did as they were told or were badly whipped.

When the galley was at sea, life on board was a living hell. From below deck came the awful sounds of chains, the cracking of whips on bare flesh, and screams of pain. At each oar, all five men had to rise as one on every stroke. They would push the eighteen-foot oar forward, dip it into the water, and pull with all their might. At the end of each stroke, they would drop back into their seats. Sometimes the

men would row like this for twenty-four hours without a minute's rest.

Nobody ever washed. Lice were everywhere. When the convicts had to row without rest, the man carrying the whip would push rolls soaked in wine into their mouths. If a convict dropped dead or fainted, he was thrown into the sea at once.

When the galley did not have to move at full speed, the convicts could rest for one and one-half hours in every three. Also a galley spent much more time in port than at sea. When in port, the convicts (all of whom had some trade) were able to get some food from the nearest town. At night they could get some much needed sleep.

1 About the Reading. Answer these questions.

1. List two ways in which people living a long time ago used the galley.

a. _____

b. _____

2. If you were going to describe the galley and what life was like on the galley to a friend, list five things you would say about it.

a. _____

b. _____

c. _____

d. _____

e. _____

3. List three things the convicts would do when the galley was in port.

a. _____

b. _____

c. _____

4. Read the first sentence. Why did people stop using the galley, and what did they use in its place? _____

_____

2 Words That Sound the Same. Put the right word on each line.

be *and* bee   **1.** The workers will _____ upset until the queen _____ returns to the hive.

know *and* no   **2.** I _____ of _____ better man for the job than Bart.

an *and* Ann   **3.** _____ had _____ hour to get all her clothes washed before she had to go to work.

throne *and* thrown   **4.** The king was _____ off his _____ when the bombs fell.

cent *and* sent   **5.** When Jim got only a one-_____-an-hour raise for all the work he had been doing, he _____ his boss a letter telling him he was going to quit.

cell *and* sell   **6.** The man in the last _____ wanted to _____ his record so he would have money for cigarettes.

hear *and* here	**7.** The mother shouted, "I could _____ you better if you came in _____ to tell me what you want."
wear *and* where	**8.** " _____ is the new gown you plan to _____ to the party?" asked Sue's sister.

3 Which Word Does Not Fit? Choose the word that doesn't fit with the rest of the words, and write it on the line to the right.

1. choose	decide	make a choice	question	_____
2. damp	dry	soaked	wet	_____
3. crowds	gangs	mobs	person	_____
4. certain	hidden	sure	true	_____
5. doze	sleep	bedroom	nap	_____
6. dream	snore	sleep	work	_____
7. billions	millions	half	thousands	_____
8. ocean	port	river	sea	_____
9. dirt	dust	mop	scrub	_____
10. grin	gripe	look pleased	smile	_____
11. battled	boxed	bumped into	fought	_____
12. gas	liquid	solid	water	_____

4 Words That Begin with *un-*. Say the words below out loud. Then put them on the lines so the sentences make sense.

unable	undress	unfolded	unmade	unsafe
unarmed	unfair	unfriendly	unprotected	untie

1. I forgot my jacket so I was _____ against the cold.

2. The string around the box was so tight that Louise couldn't _____ it.

3. As the mother looked at her child's _____ bed, she just stood there, shaking her head, and said, "I give up."

4. "Don't shoot!" shouted the bank robbers to the policemen. "We're _____."

5. The dog chained to the pole in the Joneses' front yard looked so _____ that nobody ever tried to pet him.

6. Mr. Baker wouldn't let his children play outside after dark because he felt the streets were _____.

7. Just as Joan began to _____ for bed, she remembered she had left a pot of soup on the stove.

8. Mike was _____ to go to the party on Saturday because he was running a temperature.

9. Andy wasn't looking forward to reading the letter from his girlfriend, so he _____ it very slowly.

10. When people feel sad, sometimes they think that life is _____.

5 Common Sayings. Put each word below on the right line.

away	home	ton
good	old	will
heart	thousand	worth

1. No news is _____ news.

2. You're only as _____ as you feel.

3. Where there's a _____, there's a way.

4. When the cat's _____, the mice will play.

5. It hit him like a _____ of bricks.

6. A bird in the hand is _____ two in the bush.

7. One picture is worth a _____ words.

8. Don't wear your _____ on your sleeve.

9. _____ is where the heart is.

Words for Study

George	plot	angry	creaking
Washington	bodyguard	New York	everyone
February	warning	sworn	sling
president	charge	peace	slung
kidnap	vice	countrymen	anger

The Father of Our Country

The day that we call George Washington's birthday, February 22, is not really his birthday. George Washington was born on February 11. He celebrated his first nineteen birthdays on that day. In 1752, eleven days were added to the year. This change made George Washington's birthday fall eleven days later, on February 22.

Before George Washington became president of the United States, some men tried to kidnap him in order to kill him. Their plot was found out, and one of the men turned out to be Washington's bodyguard. This man was tried before the court and found guilty. On June 8, 1776, he was hanged in a field. A crowd of 20,000 people watched. Washington hoped this would serve as a warning to others who might have the same idea in mind.

Washington hated swearing. While he was in charge of the army, he sent his men an order to stop all swearing. He called swearing a "mean and low" vice.

Washington told his men that God would hardly help them in the war against the English if they were always swearing at Him.

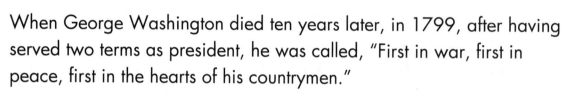

In 1782, someone told Washington that he should be king instead of president. Washington became very upset and sent the person an angry letter in which he told him never to talk like this again to anybody.

Even though George Washington was one of the richest men of his time, he had all his money tied up in land. His friends had to lend him money, so he could go to New York to be sworn in as first president of the United States.

When George Washington died ten years later, in 1799, after having served two terms as president, he was called, "First in war, first in peace, first in the hearts of his countrymen."

1 About the Reading. Answer these questions.

1. What is the real date of George Washington's birth? _____

2. On what date do we celebrate George Washington's birthday?

_____

3. What was the job of one of the men who tried to kidnap George Washington?

_____

4. Name the one thing that George Washington hated most. _____

5. In what city was George Washington sworn in as first president of the United States? _____

6. How many terms did George Washington serve as president of the United States?

_____

7. In what year did Washington become president? _____

8. Why is George Washington called the "Father of Our Country"?

_____

Do you know?

9. How many years make up a term for a president of this country? _____

10. George Washington's picture is on the _____ dollar bill.

2 Vowel Sounds. In each group of words at the left, the vowels have been changed. Say the words in each group out loud. Then put them in the right places in the sentences.

barn born burned	**1.** Mrs. King's first baby was _____ in a _____ because their house had _____ down the night before.
crack creaking crook	**2.** When the _____ stepped on the _____ in the boards, the loud _____ noise woke up everyone in the house.
tame team time	**3.** It took a long _____ for the cowboy to _____ the _____ of wild horses.
than then thin	**4.** At first George was bigger _____ John. _____ he lost 25 pounds and became very _____.
track trick truck	**5.** The _____ driver's _____ knee was hurting so badly that he lost all _____ of time.

| slang |
| sling |
| slung |

6. The stranger with his pack _____ over his back and his right arm in a _____ used so much _____ that the farmer did not know what he was talking about.

| pail |
| peeled |
| pile |

7. After all the paint had _____ off Jack's lunch _____, he threw it on the junk _____ in anger.

| stars |
| stared |
| store |

8. The lady stood at the door of her candy _____ for hours and _____ at the _____.

| whale |
| wheel |
| while |

9. _____ the man was trying to fix the steering _____ on the boat, the _____ started to swim away.

| drank |
| drinks |
| drunk |

10. The boss _____ so many _____ when he threw the birthday party for his wife that all his workers thought he'd be _____ by nine o'clock.

3 Compound Words. Find the two little words that make up each compound word, and write them on the lines to the right.

1. bodyguard _____ + _____

2. countrymen _____ + _____

3. homeless _____ + _____

4. everything _____ + _____

5. lifeboat _____ + _____

6. busybody _____ + _____

7. policeman _____ + _____

8. someone _____ + _____

9. inland _____ + _____

10. everyone _____ + _____

11. household _____ + _____

12. tablespoon _____ + _____

4 More Work with the Ending -ly. Choose a word below for each sentence.

badly	hardly	nearly	surely
friendly	lovely	really	swiftly

1. When John hit the Greens' fence, he _____ lost the whole front bumper of his car.

2. "_____ Mr. Green will sue me for the price of a new fence," thought John to himself.

3. Even during the best of times, John and Mr. Green could _____ be called good friends.

4. "Well, I might as well get this over with," mused John as he walked _____ toward the Greens' front door.

5. Mr. Green's _____ wife answered the door.

6. "I _____ feel bad about what I just did to your fence," John began.

7. "Don't sweat it," said Mrs. Green, who was always trying to be cool. "The fence was _____ in need of fixing up and painting anyway."

8. John hoped that Mr. Green would be as _____ about the whole thing as his wife was.

5 More Common Sayings. Choose a word below for each sentence.

baby	basket	candy	flies	hole	put	speak
back	boils	easy	friend	pod	say	wool

1. How time _____ when you're having fun!

2. A watched pot never _____.

3. Don't _____ all your eggs in one _____.

4. You can't pull the _____ over her eyes.

5. Everyone likes a pat on the _____ now and then.

6. Do as I _____ and not as I do.

7. A dog is man's best _____.

8. That was his ace in the _____.

9. Those twins look like two peas in a _____.

10. It was like taking _____ from a _____.

11. Don't _____ with your mouth full.

12. This reading book was as _____ as pie!

Review: Lessons 1-20

1 Words That Mean the Same. Match each word below with the word that means the same.

bold	cause	munch	peaceful	plot	utter
buddy	mad	nearly	penny	present	worthless

_____ **1.** almost

_____ **2.** angry

_____ **3.** brave

_____ **4.** calm

_____ **5.** cent

_____ **6.** chew

_____ **7.** friend

_____ **8.** gift

_____ **9.** plan

_____ **10.** reason

_____ **11.** speak

_____ **12.** useless

2 Word Opposites. Match each word below with the word that has the opposite meaning.

bold	certain	everywhere	forward	simple	spiteful
catch	deadly	fall	shrank	spicy	war

_____ **1.** back

_____ **2.** complex

_____ **3.** grew

_____ **4.** harmless

_____ **5.** kind

_____ **6.** mild

_____ **7.** not sure

_____ **8.** nowhere

_____ **9.** peace

_____ **10.** rise

_____ **11.** scared

_____ **12.** throw

3 Twenty Questions. Use the words listed below to fill in the blanks.

alphabet	Earth	galley	Pinocchio
BC	El Dorado	George Washington	pints
Black Bart	February	New Year's Day	quarts
California	forty-niners	New York	United States
doctor	Fourth of July	ounces	weigh

1. The first president of the United States was _____.

2. He went to _____ to be sworn in.

3. The first president's birthday is celebrated in the month of _____.

4. On the _____, we celebrate the time this country claimed its freedom from England.

5. _____ was a man who robbed stagecoaches and wrote poems.

6. Before the coming of steam, the _____ was the fastest boat on the inland sea.

7. The planet we live on is called _____.

8. The country we live in is called the _____.

9. The state of _____ is on the west coast of the United States.

10. The _____ went to this state in the 1840s to look for gold.

11. Long ago men looked for _____ where they hoped to find streets of gold.

12. There are four _____ in a gallon.

13. There are two _____ in a quart.

14. There are sixteen _____ in a pint.

15. The _____ begins with the letter *a* and ends with the letter *z*.

16. The letters _____ are used for dates before the birth of Christ.

17. In a well-known children's story, every time _____ told a lie, his nose grew.

18. If you get sick, a _____ can help you to be healthy again.

19. Some whales can _____ over 100 tons.

20. _____ is in the month of January.

4 Which Word Fits Best? Choose the best answer, and write it on the line.

1. Quack is to duck as bark is to _____.

   a. tree   c. pig

   b. egg   d. dog

2. Second is to minute as minute is to _____.

   a. day   c. time

   b. hour   d. week

3. Tea is to sip as gum is to _____.

   a. breathe   c. eat

   b. chew   d. sticky

4. Batter is to hitting as scribe is to _____.

   a. pen   c. teaching

   b. paper   d. writing

5. Dot is to *i* as _____ is to *t*.

   a. cross   c. print

   b. draw   d. write

6. Bike is to wheels as galleys are to _____.

   a. oars   c. steam

   b. ocean   d. whips

7. Mammals are to lungs as fish are to _____.

   a. eggs   c. gills

   b. fins   d. water

8. A penny is to one as a dime is to _____.

   a. twenty   c. ten

   b. two   d. five

9. February is to January as _____.

   a. January is to Christmas   c. March is to February

   b. June is to January   d. May is to March

10. Liquid is to solid as _____.

   a. catfish is to water   c. gold is to gold-plated

   b. cream is to coffee   d. water is to ice

5 Words That Sound the Same. Choose the right answer, and write it on the line.

threw *or* through

1. Are you glad that you are almost _____ with this reading book?

be *or* bee

2. When the president went into the store to shake hands with the voters, his bodyguard warned him to _____ careful.

cent *or* sent

3. Charles _____ his aunt a gold-plated watch for her birthday.

weak *or* week

4. After the doctor removed the cast from his leg, George felt so _____ that he was sure he would faint.

throne *or* thrown

5. After the driver had _____ down the money box from the stagecoach, Black Bart ordered him to get moving.

board *or* bored

6. Did you feel _____ when you did your homework last night?

cents *or* sense

7. While shopping for a few new things for her bathroom, Ms. Sutter said loudly, "I wouldn't give you two _____ for these ugly towels—even if they are on sale!"

way *or* weigh

8. The best time to _____ yourself is in the morning before you have had anything to eat.

brake *or* break

9. Some people have stickers on the back bumpers of their cars that read, "I _____ for animals."

know *or* no

10. Now that you are at the end of this book, do you think you _____ more about reading than you did before?

Word Index: Lessons 1–20

A
above
action
against
Alaskan
alive
allow
along
alphabet
America
anger
angry
Ann(e)
April
armchair
army
ash
ashtray
asleep
awareness
awful

B
babysit
babysitter
bail
ban
barbed
barely
Bart
basket
basketball
bathe
batter
battle
BC
beach
became
become
bee
beekeeper
beeswax
below
beluga
bend
berry
between
Bible
bigwig
billion
bird
bitter
blackbird

blink
blob
bloodstream
blouse
blown
blueberry
bluff
body
bodyguard
bold
boot
boss
Boston
bought
bouncy
boxer
brand
brand-new
bravely
break
breathe
breathing
brick
bright
bring
brink
brought
buddy
build
built
bunch
burp
bush
business
bust
busy
busybody

C
California
calves
Canada
Canadian
cancer
catbird
catfish
cattlemen
caught
cause
cave
celebration
cereal
certain
chain

change
charge
Charles
cheaply
cheek
cheesecake
chemical
chess
chessboard
chicken
children
chocolate
choice
choke
Christ
claim
claw
click
cloud
cloudless
cloudy
clue
coil
coin
colony
common
complex
compound
convict
copy
cornflakes
couch
country
countrymen
cover
cowboy
crack
cracker
craps
creak
creep
creepy
crook
crooked
crouch
crowd
crunch
crust
curse
cutters

D
dancer
dart

dash
dawn
deadly
deed
describe
deserve
diddle
dim
disease
doctor
doesn't
dollar
Donna
double
downhill
dozen
drag
drank
draw
drew
drunk
dust
dusty
dwarf

E
early
earn
Earth
easily
effect
effort
eggshell
Egypt
eighty
either
El Dorado
elm
employer
empty
endangered
energy
England
English
environment
Europe
every
everyone
everywhere
example
expert
explorer

F
factor
factory
fear
fearful
February
feeling
fence
fiddle
fiddler
field
fin
firecracker
flaky
flash
flesh
float
flood
flower
foggy
fold
folder
football
forefeet
forest
forgetful
forgot
form
forty-niner
forward
fought
fourth
Fourth of July
frame
France
freedom
freezer
fruit
fruitcake
fussily
future

G
galley
gallon
gang
Gaylord
George
gill
glitter
God
goes
gold-plated

gone
goose
grain
grand
grandstand
grapefruit
grave
graveyard
great
greed
grew
Griffiths
grin
grip
gripe
grouch
group
grow
grown
grown-up
guard
guide

H
hairless
half
handwriting
hanger
happily
health
healthy
heard
heater
heavily
heavy
he'd
helicopter
hell
he's
hey
hidden
high-class
hive
hobby
hold
holdup
homeless
honey
honeybee
hook
hopeful
horse
host
household

human
hunch
hundred

I
important
inland
instead
isn't
issue
its

J
January
Japan
Jill
Jim
John
journal
July

K
kept
kidnap
kill
king
King Solomon
kitty
kneel
knit
knitter

L
lady
lapdog
large
Las Vegas
lawful
lawn
letter
lice
lifeboat
lifetime
limb
link
lipstick
liquid
log
lonely
lord
lover
luckily

M

mainly
maker
mammal
map
March
mass
May
meaning
meaningful
meant
meatless
medical
mention
meow
microwave
middle-aged
miner
mirror
mouth
mouthful
move
mow
mower
munch

N

native
natural
nearly
necktie
needless
Nelson
nest
news
New Year's
   Day
New York
nip
noise
noisily
noisy
nonsmoking
no one
nowhere

O

ocean
order
ouch

P

pail
paper
pawn
peace
peaceful
peach
penny
pepperoni
percent
period
person
piggy
Pinocchio
pint
pipe
pizza
planet
plant
plot
poem
poet
point
pointless
police
policeman
policewoman
pollen
pollution
port
post
potato
pouch
pound
power
present
president
product
proof
protect
public
puff
punch
purr
push

Q

quart
queen

R

rail
rainbow
raise
react
reading
reason
record
recycle
reduce
refill
refrigerator
relate
remember
remove
renew
report
resource
restaurant
rhyme
rise
river
robber
robbery
round
runny
rust

S

sail
sauce
saucy
saying
says
scrap
scrape
scribe
sea
seasick
senator
sense
sentence
September
seventh
seventy
Seven Up
shack
shaky
share
sharp
sharply
shatter
shave
sheep
sheet
shell
ship
shoot
shore
shortstop
shot
shotgun
shower
shrill
sideways
sign
silent
simple
simply
sin
sister
sitter
slack
slang
slant
sleepily
sleepless
sleepy
sleeveless
slim
sling
slowly
slung
smoker
snack
snag
snap
snappy
snob
Snow White
soil
sold
solid
somebody
someone
sometimes
soundly
soup
Spain
speaker
species
spell
spice
spicy
spin
spiteful
spoil
spoke
sport
spray
spread
squid
squirt
stagecoach
stamp
stand
state
steam
stick
sticker
sticky
sting
stinger
stink
stone
stove
strand
strawberry
strip
stripe
struck
stuck
study
success
successful
suck
Sue
sue
sugar
sugarless
sugary
sunglasses
sunlight
sunshine
surely
Surgeon
   General
Sutter, J.
swell
swiftly
swimmer
swing
swipe
swizzle
sworn
swung

T

table
tablespoon
tailor
taken
tape
teabag
teach
team
teamwork
tease
teaspoon
temperature
temple
tend
term
thaw
there's
though
thoughtful
thoughtless
thousand
threat
throne
thrown
tiny
tip
tobacco
tomato
tomorrow
ton
toss
touch
touchdown
towel
tower
track
trade
trap
trapper
trash
trick
trim
trouble
troublemaker
truth
truthful
tuck
twine

U

ugly
unable
unarmed
under
underline
undress
unfair
unfold
unfriendly
United States
unmade
unprotected
untie
up-and-down
uphill
upon
useless
utter

V

vase
vegetable
Vermont
vice
vowel

W

wall
war
warm
warn
warning
wash
Washington
wasteful
watery
wavy
wax
weak
weigh
well-known
we're
whatever
whenever
wherever
whirl
whom
whose
winter
Wisconsin
wolf
wool
world
worth
worthless
worthy
wouldn't
wound
written

X

Y

yard
yawn
yellow
yolk
young

Z

zipper

Word Index: Books 1 and 2

A

a
able
about
above
according
ace
across
act
action
ad
add
address
after
afternoon
again
against
age
ago
aid
ail
air
Alaskan
alive
all
allow
all right
almost
alone
along
alphabet
also
always
am
America
amuse
amusement
an
and
Andy
anger
angry
animal
Ann(e)
another
answer
ant
any
anybody
anything
anyway
anywhere
April
are
aren't
arm
armchair
army
around
art
as
ash
ashtray
ask
asleep
at
ate
auction
aunt
awake
awareness
away
awful
awoke

B

baby
babysit
babysitter
back
bad
badge
badly
bag
bail
bake
baker
bald
ball
ban
band
bang
bank
banker
bar
barbed
bare
barely
bark
barn
Bart
base
baseball
basket
basketball
bat
batch
bath
bathe
bathroom
batter
battle
BC
be
beach
bean
bear
beat
became
because
Becky
become
bed
bedroom
bee
beef
beekeeper
been
beep
beer
beeswax
beet
before
began
begin
begun
behind
bell
below
belt
beluga
Ben
bend
bent
berry
beside
best
bet
better
between
bib
Bible
bid
big
bigwig
bike
bill
billion
Billy
bind
bird
birth
birthday
bit
bite
bitter
black
blackbird
blame
bleach
bleed
bless
blew
blind
blink
blob
block
blood
bloodstream
blouse
blow
blown
blue
blueberry
bluff
blush
board
boarder
boat
Bob
body
bodyguard
boil
bold
bolt
bomb
bond
bone
bony
book
boot
bore
born
boss
Boston
both
bought
bounce
bouncy
bow
box
boxer
boy
boyfriend
brain
brake
brand
brand-new
brave
bravely
bread
break
breakfast
breath
breathe
breathing
breathless
brick
bride
bridge
bright
bring
brink
broke
brother
brought
brown
buck
bud
buddy
bug
build
built
bulb
bull
bum
bump
bumper
bumpy
bun
bunch
bunk
bunt
burn
burp
burst
bus
bus stop
bush
business
bust
busy
busybody
but
butter
buy
by

C

cab
cage
cake
California
call
calm
calmly
calf
came
camp
can
Canada
Canadian
cancer
candy
candy bar
candy cane
cane
can't
cap
cape
Cape Cod
car
card
care
careful
careless
carry
cart
carve
case
cash
casino
cast
cat
catbird
catch
catcher
catfish
cattlemen
caught
cause
cave
ceiling
celebrate
celebration
cell
cellar
cell phone
cent
center
cereal
certain
chain
chair
chance
change
charge
Charles
charm
chart
chase
cheap
cheaply
check
checkbook
cheek
cheese
cheesecake
chemical
chess
chessboard
chest
chew
chicken
child
children
chill
chocolate
choice
choke
choose
chop
Christ
Christmas
chrome
chronic
church
cigar
cigarette
city
claim
clap
class
classroom
claw
clay
clean
cleaner
clear
click
climb
clip
clock
close
cloth
clothes
cloud
cloudless
cloudy
clown
club
clue
coach
coal
coast
coat
cod
code
coffee
coil
coin
Coke
cold
colony
comb
come
common
complex
compound
computer
cone
convict
cook
cookbook
cool
cop
cope
copper
copy
corn
cornflakes
cost
cot

couch
could
couldn't
count
country
countrymen
course
court
cousin
cover
cow
cowboy
crack
cracker
craps
crash
crawl
crazy
creak
cream
creep
creepy
crib
crime
crook
crooked
crop
cross
crouch
crowd
crown
crumb
crunch
crust
cry
cub
cube
cup
cupcake
curb
curl
curse
curtain
curve
cut
cute
cutters

D

dab
dad
dam
damp
Dan
dance
dancer
danger
Danny
dare
dark
dart
dash

date
Dave
dawn
day
daylight
dead
deadly
deal
dear
death
decide
deck
deed
deep
deer
den
dent
describe
deserve
desk
dice
Dick
did
diddle
didn't
die
dig
dim
dime
dine
diner
dining room
dinner
dip
dirt
dirty
disease
dish
ditch
dive
do
dock
doctor
dodge
does
doesn't
dog
dollar
done
donkey
Donna
don't
door
doorway
dope
dot
double
down
downhill
downstairs
downtown
doze

dozen
Dr.
drag
drain
drank
draw
dream
dress
drew
drink
drive
driver
drop
drove
drum
drunk
dry
duck
due
dues
dug
duke
dull
dumb
dump
dune
dunk
during
dusk
dust
dusty
Dutch
dwarf

E

each
ear
early
earn
Earth
easily
east
easy
eat
Eddie
eel
effect
effort
egg
eggshell
Egypt
eight
eighteen
eighty
either
El Dorado
eleven
elm
else
Elvis
employer
empty

end
endangered
energy
England
English
enough
environment
Europe
even
evening
ever
every
everybody
everyone
everything
everywhere
example
expert
explain
explorer
eye

F

face
fact
factor
factory
fad
fade
fail
faint
fair
fake
fall
false
fame
fan
fang
far
fare
farm
farmer
fast
fat
father
fear
fearful
February
fed
fee
feed
feel
feeling
feet
fell
felt
female
fence
fetch
few
fib
fiddle

fiddler
field
fifteen
fifty
fig
fight
fighter
file
fill
fin
find
fine
fire
firecracker
firm
firmly
first
fish
fist
fit
five
fix
flag
flake
flaky
flame
flare
flash
flat
flesh
flew
flip
float
flock
flood
floor
flop
flour
flow
flower
flush
fly
fog
foggy
fold
folder
fond
food
fool
foot
football
for
fore
forefeet
forest
forget
forgetful
forgot
fork
form
fortune
fortune-teller

forty
forty-niner
forward
fought
found
four
fourteen
fourth
Fourth of July
fox
frame
France
free
freedom
freeze
freezer
French
French fries
fresh
Friday
friend
friendly
from
front
froze
fruit
fruitcake
fry
fudge
full
fume
fun
fund(s)
funk
funny
fuse
fuss
fussily
fussy
future

G

galley
gallon
game
gang
gas
gate
gave
Gaylord
George
germ
get
gift
gill
gin
ginger
gingerbread
girl
girlfriend
give
glad

gland
glare
glass
gleam
glitter
glue
go
goal
God
goes
gold
gold-plated
gone
gong
good
goodness
goose
got
gotten
gown
grade
grain
grand
grandstand
grape
grapefruit
grass
grave
graveyard
gray
great
greed
green
grew
Griffiths
grill
grin
grip
gripe
groan
groom
grouch
ground
group
grow
grown
grown-up
guard
guess
guest
guide
guilt
guilty
gum
gun
guy

H

had
hadn't
hair
haircut

hairless
half
hall
ham
hammer
hand
handful
handle
handwriting
handy
hang
hanger
happen
happily
happy
hard
hardly
harm
harmful
harmless
has
hat
hate
have
haven't
hay
he
head
health
healthy
hear
heard
heart
heat
heater
heavily
heavy
heck
he'd
heel
held
helicopter
hell
hello
helmet
help
helper
helpful
helpless
hen
her
herd
here
herself
he's
hey
hi
hid
hidden
hide
high
high-class

high school
hike
hill
him
himself
hint
hip
hire
his
hit
hive
hobby
hock
hold
holdup
hole
home
homeless
homework
honey
honeybee
honk
hood
hook
hop
hope
hopeful
hopeless
horn
horse
hose
host
hot
hour
house
household
how
however
hug
huge
hum
human
hunch
hundred
hung
hunt
hunter
hurt
hut

I

I
ice
ice cream
icy
I'd
idea
if
ill
I'll
I'm
important

in
ink
inland
inside
instead
Internet
into
is
isn't
issue
it
itch
its
it's
I've

J

jab
Jack
jacket
jail
jam
January
Japan
jar
jaw
jazz
jeans
jeep
jeer
jerk
Jill
Jim
Joan
job
jobless
John
join
joint
joke
joker
Jones
jot
journal
joy
jug
July
jump
June
junk
just

K

Kate
keel
keep
keeper
kept
ketchup
key
kick
kid

kidnap
kill
kind
king
King Solomon
kiss
kit
kite
kitty
knee
kneecap
kneel
knew
knife
knit
knitter
knock
knot
know
known

L

lab
lace
lack
lady
laid
lake
lamb
lame
lamp
land
lane
lap
lapdog
laptop
large
lark
Las Vegas
last
late
later
laugh
law
lawful
lawn
lay
lead
leaf
leak
lean
learn
least
leave
led
left
leg
lend
lent
less
let
let's

letter
lice
lick
lid
lie
life
lifeboat
lifetime
lift
light
like
limb
lime
limp
line
link
lint
lip
lipstick
liquid
list
lit
little
live
load
loaf
lobby
lock
log
lone
lonely
long
look
lord
lose
lost
lot(s)
loud
loudly
Louise
love
loveliest
lovely
lover
low
loyal
luck
luckily
lucky
lug
lump
lunch
lung

M

Mack
mad
made
maid
mail
main
mainly

make
maker
male
mall
mammal
man
many
map
March
Mark
mark
marry
Mary
mask
mass
mat
match
mate
math
matter
May
may
maybe
me
meal
mean
meaning
meaningful
meant
meat
meatball
meatless
medical
meet
meeting
melt
men
mend
mention
meow
mess
messy
met
mice
microwave
middle
middle-aged
might
Mike
mild
mile
milk
million
mind
mine
miner
Min-hee
mint
minute
mirror
miss
mistake

mitt
mix
mob
mock
mole
mom
Monday
money
monkey
month
mood
moon
mop
more
morning
most
mother
mouse
mouth
mouthful
move
movie
mow
mower
Mr.
Mrs.
Ms.
much
mud
muddy
mug
muggy
mule
munch
muse
must
mute
my
myself

N

nail
name
nap
native
natural
near
nearly
neat
neck
necktie
need
needless
needy
Nelson
nerve
nest
net
never
new
news
New Year's

Day
New York
next
nice
nick
nickname
night
nine
nineteen
ninety
nip
no
nobody
nod
noise
noisily
noisy
none
noon
no one
nope
north
nose
nosy
not
note
notebook
nothing
now
nowhere
nude
numb
number
nurse
nut
nutty

O

oar
ocean
o'clock
odd
of
off
often
oh
oil
okay
old
on
once
one
online
only
open
opposite
or
order
other
ouch
ounce
our

out
outside
oven
over
own
owner

P

pace
pack
pad
page
paid
pail
pain
paint
painter
pair
pale
palm
pan
pancake
pant
pants
paper
park
parking lot
part
party
pass
past
pat
patch
path
paw
pawn
pay
paycheck
payday
payment
pea
peace
peaceful
peach
pear
peck
peek
peel
peer
pen
penny
people
pep
pepper
peppermint
pepperoni
percent
period
person
pest
pet
phone

pick
picture
pie
piece
pig
piggy
pile
pill
pin
pine
pink
Pinocchio
pint
pipe
pit
pity
pizza
place
plain
plan
plane
planet
plant
plate
play
please
plot
plug
plum
plus
pod
poem
poet
point
pointless
poke
pole
police
policeman
policewoman
pollen
pollution
pond
pool
poor
pop
popcorn
pork
pork chop
port
post
pot
potato
pouch
pound
pour
power
pray
present
president
price
pride

print
prize
problem
product
proof
protect
proud
prune
public
puff
pull
pulse
pump
punch
punt
purr
purse
push
put

Q

quack
quart
queen
question
quick
quickly
quit
quite

R

race
rack
rage
raid
rail
rain
rainbow
raincoat
raise
rake
ram
ramp
ran
rang
range
rank
rare
rat
rate
raw
reach
react
read
reading
ready
real
really
reason
record
recycle
red

reduce
reel
refill
refrigerator
refund
refuse
relate
relax
remain
remember
remind
remove
renew
rent
repay
report
resource
rest
restaurant
restroom
return
rhyme
rib
rice
rich
rid
ride
rig
right
ring
rip
ripe
rise
risk
river
road
roar
roast
roast beef
rob
robber
robbery
robe
rock
rod
rode
role
roll
room
rope
rose
rosy
rot
round
row
Roy
royal
rub
rude
rug
rule
ruler

run
rung
runny
runt
rush
rust

S

sack
sad
sadly
safe
safely
said
sail
sale
salt
same
sand
Sandy
sandy
sang
sank
sat
Saturday
sauce
saucy
save
saw
say
saying
says
scar
scare
scared
school
school bus
scooter
score
scout
scramble
scrap
scrape
scratch
scream
screech
screen
scribe
scrub
sea
search
seasick
seat
second
see
seed
seek
seem
seen
seep
self
sell

senator
send
sense
sent
sentence
September
serve
set
seven
seventeen
seventh
seventy
Seven Up
shack
shake
shaky
shame
shape
share
sharp
sharply
shatter
shave
she
sheep
sheet
shell
shift
shine
shiny
ship
shirt
shock
shook
shoot
shop
shore
short
shortstop
shot
shotgun
should
shouldn't
shout
show
shower
shrank
shred
shrill
shrimp
shrink
shrug
shrunk
shut
sick
side
sideways
sigh
sight
sign
silent
silly

simple
simply
sin
since
sing
singer
sink
sip
sister
sit
sitter
six
sixteen
sixty
skate
skill
skin
skirt
skunk
sky
slack
slam
slang
slant
slap
sleep
sleepily
sleepless
sleepy
sleeve
sleeveless
slice
slim
sling
slip
slow
slowly
slung
slush
small
smart
smash
smell
smile
smoke
smoker
snack
snag
snail
snake
snap
snappy
sneeze
snob
snore
snow
Snow White
so
soak
soap
sob
sock

socks
soft
soil
sold
solid
some
somebody
someday
someone
something
sometimes
song
soon
sore
sorry
sort
sound
soundly
soup
sour
south
space
Spain
spank
spare
spare rib
speak
speaker
species
speed
spell
spend
spent
spice
spicy
spill
spin
spite
spiteful
splash
spleen
splint
splinter
split
spoil
spoke
spoon
sport
spot
spotless
sprain
sprang
sprawl
spray
spread
spring
sprint
squash
squat
squeal
squeeze
squid

squirrel
squirt
stage
stagecoach
stain
stair
stale
stamp
stand
star
stare
start
starve
state
stay
steak
steam
steep
steer
step
stick
sticker
sticky
still
sting
stinger
stink
stomach
stone
stood
stop
store
storm
story
stove
straight
strain
strand
strange
stranger
strap
straw
strawberry
stream
street
streetlight
strict
strike
string
strip
stripe
stroke
strong
struck
struggle
stuck
study
stuff
sub
success
successful
such

suck
suddenly
suds
Sue
sue
sugar
sugarless
sugary
sum
summer
sun
sunburn
Sunday
sung
sunglasses
sunk
sunlight
sunny
sunshine
sure
surely
surf
surfer
Surgeon
    General
surprise
Sutter, J.
swear
sweat
sweater
sweet
swell
swerve
swift
swiftly
swim
swimmer
swing
swipe
switch
swizzle
sworn
swung

T

tab
table
tablespoon
tack
tail
tailor
take
taken
tale
talk
tall
tame
tan
tank
tap
tape
tar

task
taste
tax
tea
teabag
teach
teacher
team
teamwork
tear
tease
teaspoon
teeth
television
tell
teller
temper
temperature
temple
ten
tend
tent
term
test
than
that
that's
thaw
the
their
them
then
there
there's
these
they
thick
thin
thing
think
thinker
third
thirteen
thirty
this
those
though
thought
thoughtful
thoughtless
thousand
threat
three
threw
throne
through
throw
thrown
thumb
Thursday

tick
ticket
tide
tie
tight
tile
Tim
time
timeless
tin
tiny
tip
tire
to
toast
toaster
tobacco
today
told
Tom
tomato
tomorrow
ton
tone
tonight
too
took
tool
tooth
top
tore
torn
toss
touch
touchdown
toward
towel
tower
town
toy
track
trade
trail
train
trap
trapper
trash
tray
treat
tree
trick
trim
trip
trouble
troublemaker
truck
true
trunk
trust
truth
truthful
try

tub
tube
tuck
Tuesday
tug
tune
turn
TV
twelve
twenty
twice
twin
twine
twist
two

U

ugly
unable
unarmed
under
underline
undress
unfair
unfold
unfriendly
unhappy
United States
unless
unlucky
unmade
unprotected
unsafe
untie
until
unwrap
up
up-and-down
uphill
upon
upset
us
use
useful
useless
utter

V

van
vase
vegetable
Vermont
verse
very
vest
vice
voice
vote
voter
vowel

W

wade
wage
wait
wake
walk
wall
want
war
warm
warn
warning
was
wash
Washington
wasn't
waste
wasteful
watch
watchful
water
watery
wave
wavy
wax
way
we
weak
wear
web
wed
Wednesday
weed
week
weekend
weekly
weep
weigh
well
well-known
went
we're
were
west
wet
whale
what

whatever
what's
wheat
wheel
when
whenever
where
wherever
which
while
whip
whirl
white
who
whole
whom
whose
why
wide
wife
wig
wild
will
win
wind
wine
wing
wink
winner
winter
wipe
wire
wiry
Wisconsin
wish
witch
with
without
woke
wolf
woman
women
won
wonder
won't
wood
wool
word

wore
work
worker
world
worn
worry
worse
worst
worth
worthless
worthy
would
wouldn't
wound
wow
wrap
wreck
wrist
write
writer
written
wrong
wrote

X

Y

yard
yawn
year
yell
yellow
yes
yesterday
yet
yolk
you
young
you're
your
yourself

Z

zip
zipper
zone
zoo

Answer Key

Lesson 1

1 About the Reading
1. People cover their noses when they sneeze so their germs won't go all over the room.
2. When somebody sneezes, people often say, "God bless you."
3. dust, cat hair, weeds, black pepper, colds (any three)
4. 12 years old
5. 978 days
6. Answers will vary.

2 Word Sounds
1. cape
   grape
   <u>shape</u>
2. drink
   stink
   <u>think</u>
3. <u>change</u>
   range
   strange
4. chew
   <u>grew</u>
   knew
5. cries
   dries
   <u>tries</u>
6. blob
   job
   <u>snob</u>
7. grow
   <u>know</u>
   snow
8. <u>Smelling</u>
   Spelling
   Swelling
9. hand
   land
   <u>stand</u>
10. bluffed
    puffed
    <u>stuffed</u>

3 Matching
1. hearing
2. seeing
3. touching
4. tasting
5. smelling

4 Marking the e's
1. thēsҽ
2. ĕnd
3. alonҽ
4. blēed
5. harmlĕss
6. nĕxt
7. usҽful
8. pancakҽ
9. rēmind
10. swĕat
11. closҽ
12. choosҽ

5 Words That Sound the Same
1. I, eye
2. hear, here
3. Two, to
4. dear, deer
5. four, for
6. knows, nose

Lesson 2

1 About the Reading
1. United States
2. more than 90 million
3. $415,000
4. over $1,000,000
5. Cats can see better in dim light.
6. Answers will vary.

2 Word Sounds
1. brand
   grand
   <u>stand</u>
2. <u>creeps</u>
   jeeps
   beeps
3. drain
   train
   <u>brain</u>
4. wrong
   <u>strong</u>
   long
5. <u>dreaming</u>
   gleaming
   steaming
6. back
   slack
   <u>black</u>
7. brown
   clown
   <u>crown</u>
8. <u>sleep</u>
   sheep
   steep
9. seated
   heated
   <u>treated</u>
10. sends
    <u>spends</u>
    tends

3 Putting Words in Classes
List A: Cats: always land on their feet, climbing trees, meowing, nine lives, purring

List B: Dogs: barking, chasing cars, digging up bones, man's best friend, related to wolves

4 Words That Sound the Same
1. By, buy
2. knew, new
3. ate, eight
4. Do, due
5. Our, hour

Lesson 3

1 About the Reading
1. dwarves
2. Seven Up
3. the world
4. seven years
5. craps
6. You will have seven years of bad luck.

2 Word Sounds
1. blame
   <u>game</u>
   flame
2. blink
   <u>drink</u>
   stink
3. <u>Craps</u>
   Snaps
   Claps
4. blink
   drink
   <u>think</u>
5. throw
   <u>know</u>
   blow
6. knew
   <u>new</u>
   few
7. cheek
   peek
   <u>week</u>
8. bride
   <u>pride</u>
   hide
9. <u>place</u>
   face
   race

3 Number Words
1. twenty-four
2. thirty-one
3. thirty
4. fifty
5. forty
6. Answers will vary.
7. Answers will vary, depending on state law.
8. eighteen

4 Word Opposites
1. go
2. many
3. break
4. soft
5. win
6. everybody
7. something
8. in

Lesson 4

1 About the Reading
1. three billion
2. pepperoni
3. Japan
4. 140 pounds
5. Half are fresh and half are in foods like French fries.
6. one pound of cheese
7. popcorn
8. strawberries
9. ketchup or tomato sauce
10. grapes
11. Answers will vary.
12. Answers will vary.

2 Word Sounds
1. change
   range
   <u>strange</u>
2. post
   <u>most</u>
   host
3. scream
   dream
   <u>cream</u>
4. found
   <u>pound</u>
   sound
5. <u>filled</u>
   spilled
   killed
6. sheet
   street
   <u>sweet</u>
7. chew
   <u>threw</u>
   blew
8. prices
   spices
   <u>slices</u>

3 Word Sounds
1. stairs, pair, chairs
2. proud, cloud, loudly
3. brave, waves, cave
4. cried, tried, dried
5. hear, clear, near
6. range, change, strange
7. mean, beans, jeans
8. lunch, munched, bunch
9. trick, bricks, stick
10. shape, cape, grape

4 Compound Words

1. pop + corn
2. fruit + cake
3. break + fast
4. out + side
5. blue + berries
6. grape + fruit
7. straw + berry
8. some + body
9. every + where
10. cook + book

5 Which Word Does Not Fit?

1. snack
2. pear
3. candy
4. world
5. pets
6. pound
7. mall

6 Smallest and Biggest

1. week — year
2. thousand — billion
3. grape — potato
4. Japan — world
5. third — whole
6. none — many
7. baby — grown-up
8. ounce — ton

Lesson 5

1 About the Reading

1. 1875
2. scribe
3. 1,875,000
4. 2,010,000
5. Answers will vary.
6. Answers will vary. Acceptable answers include that people did not have phones or the Internet and that visiting people who lived some distance away was more difficult in the 1800's than it is today.

2 Word Sounds

1. telling
2. passed
3. mail
4. life
5. six
6. more
7. vowels
8. such
9. still
10. song

3 Who Does What?

1. cab driver
2. baseball player
3. teacher
4. doctor
5. cowboy
6. tailor
7. clown
8. painter
9. lover
10. scribe

4 Words That Sound the Same

1. write, right
2. whole, hole
3. beat, beet
4. fare, fair
5. meet, meat
6. heard, herd
7. sale, sails
8. won, one

5 Marking the Vowels

1. frāmé
2. brănd
3. knōwn
4. pīnt
5. stāté
6. sĭns
7. sĕnsé
8. cătbĭrd
9. squĭd
10. rēlāté
11. spīcé
12. wrōté

Review: Lessons 1–5

1 Choosing the Answer

1. fifty
2. talk
3. sense
4. lace
5. mate
6. mean
7. blob
8. blushing
9. renew
10. deadly

2 Number Words

1. seven
2. fifty-two
3. sixteen
4. eight
5. two
6. two
7. four
8. thirteen
9. fifty
10. seven
11. Answers will vary.
12. One thousand

3 Facts

1. sight
2. hearing
3. taste
4. touch
5. smell

Lesson 6

1 About the Reading

1. wool, animal hair, gold
2. beeswax
3. He began to lose his hair at an early age.
4. These wigs were huge, covering people's backs and hanging down over their chests.
5. 12 years
6. Many years ago in Egypt, the bigger a person's wig was, the more important the person was.
7. Answers will vary.

2 Word Sounds

1. shave
2. bangs
3. hair
4. throne
5. which
6. Feeling
7. Fighting
8. bugs
9. stand

3 Which Word Does Not Fit?

1. month
2. English
3. catbird
4. scribe
5. start
6. Anne
7. queen
8. wrist
9. well
10. pound

4 Vowel Sounds

Long Sound for *ea*

1. bean
2. beat
3. easy
4. please
5. squeal

Short Sound for *ea*

1. bread
2. breakfast
3. dead
4. instead
5. sweat

5 Compound Words

1. bath + room
2. big + wig
3. cow + boy
4. cat + bird
5. check + book
6. some + one
7. ginger + bread
8. girl + friend
9. short + stop
10. sun + light

Lesson 7

1 About the Reading

1. The liquid comes from two pouches under the skunk's tail.
2. A skunk can spray his liquid from a range of ten to twelve feet.
3. He has to wait a few days before he can spray again.
4. A skunk sprays his liquid to ward off danger.
5. He faces whatever he thinks is chasing him.
   a. He stamps his forefeet.
   b. He raises all but the tip of his tail.
   c. He raises the tip of his tail and sprays his liquid.
6. Answers will vary.

2 Compound Words

1. bed + room
2. blood + stream
3. trouble + maker
4. home + work
5. tea + bag
6. note + book
7. side + ways
8. some + one
9. cat + fish
10. what + ever

3 Words That Mean the Same

1. wreck
2. hidden
3. creep
4. sprint
5. touch
6. bluff
7. nice
8. build
9. trouble
10. grin

4 Word Opposites

1. old	4. nothing	7. shut	9. saved
2. late	5. shrink	8. forget	10. lovely
3. hard	6. find		

5 Silly Verses

1. state, straight, sky, cry, dates
2. France, pants, tried, cried, dance
3. sour, hour, life *or* wife, life *or* wife, shower

Lesson 8

1 About the Reading

1. 75 billion
2. 24–26 hours
3. about 256
4. Answers will vary.
5. tiny holes
6. Water and gas move through the holes in the eggshell.
7. They can blow up.
8. about three weeks
9. Put the egg in saltwater and see if it sinks.
10. Answers will vary.

2 Word Sounds

1. lay	4. bite	7. bust	9. cared
pay	kite	dust	glared
say	white	just	scared
2. shell	5. brains	8. choke	10. years
smell	grains	spoke	clears
spell	chains	broke	fears
3. spin	6. fail		
grin	mail		
thin	pail		

3 Word Sounds

Book		School	
1. foot	4. wood	1. groom	4. spoon
2. hood	5. wool	2. pool	5. tooth
3. took		3. shoot	

4 Which Word Fits Best?

1. glass	4. chill	7. chair	9. school
2. sky	5. England	8. foot	10. lung
3. pack	6. Wednesday		

5 Compound Words

1. armchair	4. forefeet	7. rainbow
2. babysit	5. grandstand	8. sometimes
3. eggshell	6. lifetime	9. touchdown

1. touchdown	4. grandstand	7. babysit
2. eggshell	5. armchair	8. rainbow
3. Sometimes	6. forefeet	9. lifetime

Lesson 9

1 About the Reading

1. California
2. John Sutter
3. 1849
4. forty-niners
5. one ounce
6. They were lonely and there were few women around.
7. Answers will vary.

2 Word Sounds

1. bread	3. blind	5. leans	7. shores
dead	find	cleans	stores
spread	mind	means	scores
2. bought	4. fool's	6. cold	8. free
fought	cool's	gold	tree
thought	pool's	hold	three

3 Vowels + the Letter *l*

1. belt	4. milk	7. wall	10. bald
2. tall	5. gold	8. bell	11. Jill, hill
3. roll	6. bulb	9. cold	

4 Marking the Vowels

1. līcé	6. rēason	11. Fránce	15. hălf
2. kěpt	7. rāisé	12. brāké	16. tǐp
3. dăsh	8. grāvé	13. betwēēn	17. sǐncé
4. glǐtter	9. chēēk	14. jŭst	18. brēathé
5. flōat	10. těst		

5 Matching

1. coffee	5. yolk	8. lice
2. peach	6. March	9. news
3. chocolate	7. kneel	10. microwave
4. bigwig		

Lesson 10

1 About the Reading

1. Boston
2. 1760
3. No
4. to carry soup
5. to taste the soup before the queen tried it
6. They ran off to get married.
7. The rhymes had been around for hundreds of years before they were called Mother Goose rhymes.
8. Answers will vary.

2 Word Sounds

1. born	4. bed	7. door	9. cane
corn	fed	poor	plane
horn	red	floor	lane
2. die	5. feet	8. knee	10. drum
pie	sheet	three	plum
tie	street	bee	gum
3. close	6. block		
nose	clock		
rose	shock		

3 Which Word Does Not Fit?

1. California	5. car	9. air	12. smoker
2. snow	6. leaves	10. wool	13. beach
3. spring	7. ice	11. cowboys	14. punt
4. pound	8. straw		

4 Silent Letters

1. knit	4. claim	7. wrist	10. heart
2. breath	5. wrong	8. climb	11. lamb
3. fetch	6. thumb	9. meant	12. watch

5 Words That Sound the Same

1. red, read
2. see, sea
3. weak, week
4. through, threw
5. bear, bare
6. way, weigh
7. break, brake
8. sense, cents

Review: Lessons 1–10

1 Choosing the Answer

1. soundly
2. though
3. peered
4. burp
5. six
6. main
7. spoil
8. guess
9. hunch

2 Words That Mean the Same

1. shut
2. glitter
3. tease
4. guide
5. spoil
6. break
7. dirt
8. brake
9. melt
10. slim
11. rhyme
12. during

3 Word Opposites

1. dirty
2. cloudy
3. rare
4. sink
5. against
6. thaw
7. evening
8. neat
9. forgot
10. crooked
11. weak
12. lies

Lesson 11

1 About the Reading

1. We are trying to draw in more air.
2. a. Body heat goes down.
   b. Brain waves become more even.
3. a. The heart rate slows down.
   b. The body relaxes.
   c. Breathing becomes very even.
4. Most dreaming happens during the deepest stage of sleep called REM.
5. It would take me quite a few seconds to move.
6. I would probably become very sick.
7. Answers will vary.
8. Answers will vary.

2 Word Sounds

1. paws, claws
2. thaws, straw
3. jaw, law
4. dawn, lawn
5. pawns, yawn
6. lawful, awful

3 Long and Short Vowels

1. breathe, breath
2. bathe, bath
3. tap, tape
4. scrap, scrape
5. gripe, grip
6. twin, twine

4 Putting Words in Order

1. Mr. White couldn't go to sleep.
2. First he tried counting sheep.
3. Then he fixed himself a cup of tea.
4. He still couldn't fall asleep.
5. The next day he was fired for sleeping on the job.

Lesson 12

1 About the Reading

1. about 30 million years
2. about 10,000
3. nine
4. $15 billion
5. They carry pollen from one tree to another.
6. honey and beeswax
7. colonies
8. Bee colonies began dying.
9. in a few weeks
10. pests, disease, what the bees eat, chemicals, or a mix of problems (any one)
11. no
12. There wouldn't be as many bees to help fruit grow.

2 Word Sounds

1. miles
2. five
3. die
4. stripes
5. flowers
6. honey
7. must
8. more
9. give

3 Words That End in -y

1. sleepy
2. watery
3. sticky
4. sugary
5. creepy
6. worthy

1. sunny
2. snappy
3. piggy
4. kitty
5. buddy
6. foggy

1. spicy
2. shiny
3. noisy
4. saucy
5. shaky
6. wavy

4 Words That End in -ly

1. quickly
2. Simply
3. sharply
4. calmly
5. barely
6. bravely
7. cheaply
8. lonely
9. nearly
10. weekly

5 Compound Words

1. beeswax
2. afternoon
3. seasick
4. teaspoon
5. honeybee
6. teamwork
7. beekeepers
8. Whenever

6 Changing the f to v

1. leaves
2. wives
3. knives
4. wolves
5. dwarves
6. selves
7. halves
8. lives

Lesson 13

1 About the Reading

1. a. He looks at the slant.
   b. He studies the direction of the writing line.
   c. He studies the size and width of the letters.
2. a. false
   b. true
   c. true
   d. false
   e. false
   f. true
3–5. Answers will vary.

2 Words That Mean the Same

1. shirt
2. large
3. barely
4. allow
5. bright
6. certain
7. present
8. double
9. marry
10. scream

3 Word Opposites

1. asleep
2. sunny
3. birth
4. uphill
5. bright
6. begin
7. won
8. young
9. yesterday
10. summer

4 Vowel Sounds

Star	Air	Ear
1. are	1. bear	1. beer
2. carve	2. fair	2. dear
3. hard	3. stare	3. deer
4. heart	4. their	4. here
5. march	5. wear	5. peer

Lesson 14

1 About the Reading

1. as early as 1000 BC
2. in the Americas
3. They chewed or smoked them.
4. in the late 1400s
5. in the mid-1500s
6. 1856
7. It rolled the tobacco in paper.
8. cigarette ads
9. Answers will vary.
10. Answers will vary.

2 True or False?

1. false	4. true	7. false
2. true	5. true	8. true
3. false	6. false	

3 Working with Words That Rhyme

1. door, for, pour, more
2. rest, nest, best, test
3. street, meet, seat, beat
4. sky, dry, try, tie
5. tent, bent, went, rent

4 Words That End in -er

1. sticker	1. smoker	1. trapper
2. hanger	2. driver	2. batter
3. heater	3. maker	3. slimmer
4. cracker	4. dancer	4. zipper
5. mower	5. freezer	5. swimmer

Lesson 15

1 About the Reading

1. Hold Fast, Saw Tooth, Wrap Around, Brink Twist, Necktie (any three)
2. He gold-plated swizzle sticks and sold them to a big store.
3. Their main goal is to own at least one strand of every kind of barbed wire ever made.
4. the way they looked.
5. a. The doctor gets into his helicopter.
   b. He flies over miles of fence looking for barbed wire.
   c. He sees something that looks good.
   d. He sets his helicopter down in a field.
   e. He takes out his wire cutters and cuts off a strand.
6. farmers
7. Possible answer: They used it to keep cattle away from their crops.

2 Working with Words That Rhyme

1. cold, gold, folded, sold
2. brink, drink, sink, stink
3. grand, strand, land, brand
4. Mack, rack, lacked, sack
5. cared, share, bare, spare
6. Sutter, utter, cutters, butter
7. tucked, stuck, sucked, luck
8. king, bring, sting, sing
9. wiped, griped, swiped, ripe
10. crook, look, hook, book

3 How Do You Say It?

1. flock	5. pack	9. bunch	13. bar
2. loaf	6. pot	10. quart	14. book
3. deck	7. herd	11. pair	15. load
4. box	8. school	12. can	

Review: Lessons 1–15

1 Choosing the Answer

1. sticky	6. crosses	11. grape
2. flaky	7. nowhere	12. hobby
3. foggy	8. grouches	13. Fourth of July
4. repaid	9. batter	14. North and the South
5. filed	10. bid	

2 Silent Letters

1. wrote	5. young	9. batch
2. dumb	6. build	10. writer
3. badge	7. knee	11. witch
4. Dutch	8. dodge	12. certain

3 Matching

1. rainbow	4. towel	7. alphabet	9. wax
2. oven	5. fence	8. piggy	10. pepper
3. mower	6. stamp		

4 Word Sounds

1. whose	3. allow	5. soup	7. flood
2. certain	4. bath	6. heading	8. ginger

5 Compound Words

1. lipstick	5. firecrackers	8. cheesecake
2. babysitter	6. policewoman	9. underline
3. sunglasses	7. stagecoach	10. busybody
4. ashtray		

Lesson 16

1 About the Reading

1. more than forty
2. the blue whale
3. 100 feet or as long as a basketball court
4. in the 1800s
5. a. hunting ocean mammals in United States waters
   b. products made from whales
6. It protects rare plants and animals.
7. eight
8. beluga whale

9. Alaska
10. pollution, boats, noise (any two)
11. California gray whale
12. about 21,000
13. 1993
14. Answers will vary.

2 True or False?
1. true
2. false
3. false
4. false
5. false
6. true
7. false
8. true
9. true
10. false

3 Putting Words in Order
1. I once saw a whale in Canada.
2. Sue had breakfast with her friends on her birthday.
3. Becky took a bike ride on Friday.
4. Andy plays basketball with his dad.
5. A bug bit my arm on Tuesday.

4 Changing the -y to -i
1. bumpier   bumpiest
2. dirtier   dirtiest
3. easier   easiest
4. friendlier   friendliest
5. funnier   funniest
6. happier   happiest
7. needier   neediest
8. guiltier   guiltiest
9. muddier   muddiest
10. healthier   healthiest

5 More Work with Changing the -y to -i
1. happily
2. fussily
3. noisily
4. sleepily
5. Luckily
6. easily

6 Which Word Fits Best?
1. people
2. mammal
3. find
4. horses
5. flower
6. football
7. cow
8. wood
9. tomorrow
10. nowhere

Lesson 17

1 About the Reading
1. Charles
2. eight years
3. more than thirty
4. teaching
5. about two thousand dollars
6. He intended only to scare the driver.
7. a. He made careful plans.
   b. He always worked alone.
   c. He never held up stagecoaches near home.
   d. He never told anyone about his plans.
8. A teacher earned about one thousand dollars a year.
9. because he was a poet
10. Answers may vary.

2 Words That Mean the Same
1. limbs
2. earn
3. clue
4. robbery
5. alive
6. all right
7. verse
8. cause
9. high-class
10. strip

3 Word Opposites
1. under
2. dozed
3. scared
4. full
5. awful
6. harmful
7. leave
8. fresh
9. froze
10. cool

4 A Verse from Black Bart
bread, chance, dead, able, blame, curses, hung, verses

5 The Ending -ful
1. successful
2. truthful
3. mouthful
4. thoughtful
5. fearful
6. meaningful
7. forgetful
8. hopeful
9. wasteful
10. spiteful

Lesson 18

1 About the Reading
1. April 22
2. to raise awareness of environmental issues
3. in towns, businesses, schools, and everywhere
4. Answers will vary.

2 Word Sounds
1. sprinted, spray, sprawled, sprained
2. stranger, strong, streets, strike
3. swung, swiftly, swimming, switch, swinging
4. scraped, screen, screamed, scrubbing
5. squirrel, squeezed, squirt
6. strained, straight, struck, stroke

3 The Ending -less
1. sleeveless
2. breathless
3. sleepless
4. sugarless
5. thoughtless
6. worthless
7. meatless
8. cloudless
9. useless
10. pointless
11. hairless
12. Needless

4 Same or Opposite?
1. same
2. same
3. opposite
4. opposite
5. opposite
6. same
7. same
8. opposite
9. opposite
10. same
11. opposite
12. same
13. opposite
14. opposite

5 Spelling Check
1. March
2. empty
3. Earth
4. stork
5. January
6. nerve
7. mammal
8. pollution
9. rainbow
10. cheese

Lesson 19

1 About the Reading
1. a. They used galleys to guard the coast.
   b. They used galleys to remove ships wounded in battle.
2. Note: The details below may be listed in any order. Other details may be included as well.
   a. The galley was mainly an open boat for four hundred men.
   b. Convicts manned the oars that made the galley move swiftly.

c. Each oar was manned by five convicts.

d. Sometimes the convicts rowed for twenty-four hours without any rest.

e. Nobody ever washed.

3. a. They would work at their respective trades.

   b. They would get some food from the nearest town.

   c. They would get much-needed sleep.

4. They used steam when it became available because it was faster.

2 Words That Sound the Same

1. be, bee
2. know, no
3. Ann, an
4. thrown, throne
5. cent, sent
6. cell, sell
7. hear, here
8. Where, wear

3 Which Word Does Not Fit?

1. question
2. dry
3. person
4. hidden
5. bedroom
6. work
7. half
8. port
9. dirt
10. gripe
11. bumped into
12. water

4 Words That Begin with *un-*

1. unprotected
2. untie
3. unmade
4. unarmed
5. unfriendly
6. unsafe
7. undress
8. unable
9. unfolded
10. unfair

5 Common Sayings

1. good
2. old
3. will
4. away
5. ton
6. worth
7. thousand
8. heart
9. Home

Lesson 20

1 About the Reading

1. February 11
2. February 22 or on President's Day
3. his bodyguard
4. swearing
5. New York City
6. two
7. 1789
8. He was the first president of the United States. He commanded the Continental Army in its effort to gain independence from England. He also served as president of the convention that wrote the Constitution.
9. four years
10. one

2 Vowel Sounds

1. born, barn, burned
2. crook, crack, creaking
3. time, tame, team
4. than, Then, thin
5. truck, trick, track
6. slung, sling, slang
7. peeled, pail, pile
8. store, stared, stars
9. While, wheel, whale
10. drank, drinks, drunk

3 Compound Words

1. body + guard
2. country + men
3. home + less
4. every + thing
5. life + boat
6. busy + body
7. police + man
8. some + one
9. in + land
10. every + one
11. house + hold
12. table + spoon

4 More Work with the Ending *-ly*

1. nearly
2. Surely
3. hardly
4. swiftly
5. lovely
6. really
7. badly
8. friendly

5 More Common Sayings

1. flies
2. boils
3. put, basket
4. wool
5. back
6. say
7. friend
8. hole
9. pod
10. candy, baby
11. speak
12. easy

Review: Lessons 1–20

1 Words That Mean the Same

1. nearly
2. mad
3. bold
4. peaceful
5. penny
6. munch
7. buddy
8. present
9. plot
10. cause
11. utter
12. worthless

2 Word Opposites

1. forward
2. simple
3. shrank
4. deadly
5. spiteful
6. spicy
7. certain
8. everywhere
9. war
10. fall
11. bold
12. catch

3 Twenty Questions

1. George Washington
2. New York
3. February
4. Fourth of July
5. Black Bart
6. galley
7. Earth
8. United States
9. California
10. forty-niners
11. El Dorado
12. quarts
13. pints
14. ounces
15. alphabet
16. BC
17. Pinocchio
18. doctor
19. weigh
20. New Year's Day

4 Which Word Fits Best?

1. dog
2. hour
3. chew
4. writing
5. cross
6. oars
7. gills
8. ten
9. March is to February
10. water is to ice

5 Words That Sound the Same

1. through
2. be
3. sent
4. weak
5. thrown
6. bored
7. cents
8. weigh
9. brake
10. know

Challenger SECOND EDITION
ADULT READING SERIES
2

Challenger's eight levels guide adult learners from beginning reading through to preparing for the GED. Challenger uses phonics, controlled vocabulary, and sequential skill development. Skills and concepts are presented in the context of diverse fiction and nonfiction passages relevant to adults.

READING LEVEL 1–2
phonics charts, original story themes include relationships, jobs, online shopping, gambling, and night school

READING LEVEL 2–3
nonfiction article topics include food facts, lucky number 7, animals, smoking, and Earth Day

READING LEVEL 3–4.5
phonics charts, original story themes include yoga, friendship, e-mail, interactive video games, healthy food

READING LEVEL 4–5
nonfiction article topics include Danica Patrick, energy crisis, cell phones, internet dating, cloning, and digestion

READING LEVEL 4.5–5.5
phonics charts, mainly fiction, short stories, myths, fables including family secrets, The Death of King Arthur, a science fiction story, O. Henry short stories

READING LEVEL 5.5–6.5
Themed Units: Family (healthy food, multiracial family, caring for elderly family members), Getting a Job, Going Places, and Food

READING LEVEL 6.5–7.5
phonics charts, Themed Units: Love and Money, Struggle, Fantasy vs. Reality (stories by Saki, Ambrose Bierce, Lewis Carroll, and others), Brushes with Death, Giving

READING LEVEL 7.5–9
Themed Units: Appearances (celebrity vs. reality), Explorers (Marco Polo to space exploration), The Good Earth (includes rainforests and deforestation), Change (Obama)

Writing Books 1–8 Include instruction and practice in mechanics, grammar, organization, transitions, and other writing skills. Two-page writing lessons guide students from writing simple sentences through to writing 5-paragraph essays.

Teacher's Manuals 1–4 & 5–8 Include scope & sequence charts, lesson planning, revising and editing checklists, lesson notes, extension activities, and writing book answer keys.

New Readers Press
ProLiteracy's publishing division
Syracuse, New York
800-448-8878
www.newreaderspress.com

ISBN 978-1-56420-569-8

9 781564 205698